LOVING HENRY

HENRY

KATE LAWSON

EOS

PUBLISHING

Dedication

For my darling wife, who had the upmost patience with me while I spent countless hours typing away, and to my mother, who I know will read far more into this than necessary.

ABOUT THE AUTHOR

Website:
http://eos-publishing.com/kate-lawson
Twitter:
https://twitter.com/lawson_writes
Facebook:
https://www.facebook.com/maydawney
Instagram:
https://www.instagram.com/maydawney

ABOUT EOS PUBLISHING

Website:
http://eos-publishing.com
Twitter:
https://twitter.com/eospublishing
Facebook:
https://www.facebook.com/eospublishing
Instagram:
http://instagram.com/eospublishing

SUBSCRIBE TO NEWSLETTER

https://eos-publishing.com/newsletter

Rachel

THE FIRST TIME it happened, she was waiting for Andy to emerge from the toilets at St Pancras station. While it was raining outside, they had yet to encounter it since their arrival into London, the train pulling straight into the wrought iron building and under the artificial light. The shops they'd passed as Andy rushed them to the loos could have placed them anywhere in the world, only the robotic voice of the woman announcing train departures and arrivals placed them in the capital.

Rachel had leant against one of the cold plastic-coated walls as she waited for her friend and called her brother to confirm where they were going to meet. He'd instantly started prattling on about something or other; from the odd words she caught, she thought one of the kids had been sick on the drive down. Rachel wasn't listening. At first she had nodded along, making appreciative noises at all the right intervals, she even convinced herself she was doing an excellent job of feigning interest in whatever he was talking about, but then her eyes fell onto the teenager.

The boy stood barely five metres away from her, his back against the shop window and his hands in his pockets, displayed like the mannequins on the other side of the glass. His thick winter coat didn't quite fit him; it hung loosely, waiting for him to grow into it, and revealed a football shirt beneath. He would have been entirely unremarkable but for the fact that he was staring at her. Even when she caught his eyes, his did not deviate, he simply continued to watch her as she tried to maintain the façade of listening to her brother talking at her from the other end of the phone.

As the teenager continued to watch her, Rachel instinctively touched her hair, tucking strays behind her ear, as if that would stop the boy from staring. She pinned the phone between her ear and shoulder so both hands could attend to her face, one wiping her mouth with its back, the other gravitating to her eyes. She looked around the space for a mirror, wondering what had this stranger watching her so intently. Finding none, she zipped up her jacket, obscuring the—what she deemed to be, at least—inoffensive message of her sweatshirt. But the boy's eyes continued to press her, pinning her to the wall she was leaning on.

Her phone rang, sending vibrations through her head, forcing her attention back to where it should have been all along: Luke. She took it back into her hand and stared at it blankly. Her brother was now FaceTiming her.

Her eyes flickered between the screen and the boy. He continued to watch her. He was waiting for her to answer the phone, just as her brother was.

She clicked the green button and Luke's face filled the screen, annoyance written across his features. All she could offer in return was an apologetic smile; she could hardly explain the discomfort of a stranger's staring to herself, let alone try and vocalise it to Luke.

"When did you stop listening to me?" he demanded, before carrying on regardless. "It doesn't matter. We're at the museum already. How long do you think you'll be?"

"I'm just waiting for Andy," Rachel told him. "She's peeing, then we need to figure out the Tube."

She looked back to the boy, needing to know why he was staring so intently, but his eyes had finally moved away from her. There was a man with him who looked ten, possibly fifteen years older than herself. He held a small boy wearing the colours of the same football team, the red of his shirt radiating brightly off the brown of his skin.

The man said something, but the teenager was on his phone, paying the man as much attention as Rachel was to her brother.

It was only Andy's arrival that pulled her away and back to her conversation.

"She's here now, we'll see you in a bit." Rachel closed the call without any fanfare. "Luke," she explained to Andy as she pocketed her mobile, knowing the boy was watching her every movement once again.

"It's only fifteen minutes on the Piccadilly, drop him a text before your signal goes."

Andy waited for Rachel to make some sort of movement towards her. Gingerly, Rachel pulled away from her sanctuary against the wall. Her face reddening under the pressure of the teenager's eyes upon her as she tried, in vain, not to look back.

Yet she did. She had to.

The family had been joined by a woman—logic dictated that she must be the mother—who was complaining loudly about the state of the women's toilets and the length of the queue in comparison to the men's.

As Rachel passed them, she felt fingers wrap around her left arm, it pulled her back to the teenager and his unrelenting gaze that she was trying so diligently to ignore, trying in earnest yet failing all the same.

"I'm sorry," the teenager said quietly, meeting her eyes—blue, flecks of brown, in stark contrast to the red shirt of his football team. "Do I know you?"

"No."

She pulled her arm free and caught up with Andy. If only she hadnt't looked back, she might have been spared the confrontation. If only she were braver, she could have said something, told the child off for making her feel so alien and unwanted, demanded an apology for his actions.

"What was that about?" Her friend frowned.

Rachel could only shrug; she still hadn't found the words to articulate what she was feeling.

"You all right?"

There were so many answers to that question: she knew she was far from alright, the boy had been staring at her as if he knew all her secrets, as if she didn't belong, as if standing there were a sin. She shook her head free of him. "Yeah, come on, let's do science." Rachel forced a smile to cross her lips as she led Andy down into the Underground.

* * *

The second time she saw him was on the train heading home. They'd purposely arrived early so they could sit at a table. Andy flicked through a book she'd picked up from the museum's gift shop. Rachel had bought trinkets for her niece and nephew but nothing for herself, so, with only her phone to occupy her, she found herself people watching.

She saw shoppers, commuters, and tourists all pour onto the train and then watched as a family and the teenager climbed on after them.

She had first seen him at St Pancras, it seemed logical that it would be there she might see him again. It did, however, feel somewhat near impossible that he would board her train and head in the same direction—back to Kent—with her. If she were a mathematician, she might have been able to calculate the odds, yet maths had never been her strong point, and such was the feeling of dread that had settled on the tops of her shoulders, the coldness of it making her feel sick; she doubted she would be able to accomplish anything, least of all sums. She scanned the carriage frantically before resigning herself to the fact that they would sit at the table behind Andy, that the teenager would sit, that he would see her, and his unrelenting eyes would watch her for the duration of their shared journey.

"Swap seats!" Rachel stood in such a hurry that she banged her thighs on the table. When Andy made no movement, her face only showing shades of annoyance mixed with the inevitable tiredness that comes from a day of travelling and the forced joviality spent with someone else's family, Rachel tried again. "I'm facing backwards, I can't travel backwards."

"You did all right on the ride up here."

"The train was crowded, I had no choice." Why wasn't she just telling her best friend the truth, that a teenager, *the* teenager, had boarded their train and made her uncomfortable? That he'd stared at her before and she was worried he'd stare again. That she didn't have the courage to confront him in case the parents told her off— because they undoubtedly would. A stranger starts yelling at their child, they would yell back in his defence—she'd played the whole scene out in her head and found the only way to escape from it all was to hide.

"Just sit next to me and stop fussing." Andy returned her attention to the book in front of her.

"I don't—"

"For fuck's sake, just sit down. I work with five-year-olds that can demonstrate greater maturity than you at the moment."

Rachel could only slump into the seat beside her and hope she'd moved fast enough for the family not to have noticed her. But she was on the aisle, so her chances were slim.

"Better?" Andy asked. Rachel only grunted a response. "Suit yourself."

The family had, as predicted, chosen to settle into the adjacent table, and she was able to observe their reflection in the window.

If it had been earlier, the evening light would have been too strong to transform the windows into mirrors. But if it had been earlier, they would have caught different trains. If it had been earlier, she wouldn't have seen the teenager again.

Rachel felt her chair move as the parents took the seats behind her, and she heard the younger son's excitement as he recounted the game to them all. Mispronounced surnames were stumbled upon one after the other, before the father finally interjected. "Those boys weren't a patch on Clough's Forest."

"Yes, dear," the mother drawled out tiredly, "we all know you're from Nottingham." Rachel heard the teenager struggle to stifle his laugh. "Why you can't all enjoy a nice summer sport rather than sitting out in the cold for two hours just to complain about an inane refereeing decision for the next week, I'll never understand."

"Mum"—she could hear the remnants of his smile in the teenager's voice—"you're never going to persuade me to go to one of your horse shows."

"Luckily for you, I have Caitlin."

"Perhaps," the father sounded almost timid in his suggestion, "we three men could go camping the next time Caitlin takes your mother to Wales for a show."

"I go camping with Pops."

"Henry"—*Henry*. The teenager's name was Henry—"don't be rude."

"It's quite all right," the father quashed the mother's reproach. "It's understandable that he would want to spend time with his namesake."

"Still."

Rachel couldn't quite catch the rest of the interaction as their voices dropped below a whisper. No doubt a discussion of meaningful looks and eye rolls, the kind acquired after years spent in one another's company. She wanted so desperately to hear what they were saying, as if the discussion between the parents might be able to explain the actions of their son, that she might be allowed a reason for his staring. But all she could hear was the sound of the train, the wiring of the electrics that powered it, the rattling of the seats, a distant beat of someone else's music ringing too loudly in their ears.

Yet only silence surrounded the family.

She chanced another glance at the window and another look at him. The teenager had his phone out again, and the young boy had been given some colouring pencils and a book. All she could see of the parents were his fingers picking at his nails; she imagined the mother's arms to be folded tightly across her chest.

As the train pulled out of St Pancras and took them back to Kent, she felt Andy's head drop onto her shoulder.

"Where are you?" she asked quietly.

"Right here." Rachel smiled weakly back at her.

She pulled out her phone and a set of headphones, intending to listen to music or a podcast whilst Andy slept on her shoulder. The warmth of the girl on her shoulders, the familiarity of it, reduced everything else she was feeling to nothingness. She wanted to wrap her arm around Andy, pull her in closer, but she fought the urge, fearing her friend's wrath—touching in public was forbidden.

Instead Rachel stared out of the window, never getting around to pressing play.

She envisioned the journey before them: The city would fall to fields, and in an hour and five minutes she would return to the flat she shared with Andy. They would pretend to argue about who was going to cook dinner (knowing Andy would do it). They would watch TV or something on Netflix, go to their beds, make sure their alarms were set, and wake up for work tomorrow. Everything would be as it was, and this day wouldn't matter. These two sightings of the teenager would be inconsequential, the memory could become a dream and, perhaps, the encounter might never have happened at all.

Thirty-eight minutes passed, and the family alighted at Ashford. This station was open and exposed to the world, the darkness of the autumn night mixed with the strip lighting of a modern station. Rachel watched them go, the teenager following his parents down the platform and towards the stairs that would take them to the exit, hands deep in his pockets, headphones still in his ears. Then he stopped and turned back to the train. Their eyes met again. Blue, flecks of brown. He was too far away for her to read his expression clearly, but even with the distance it was obvious he'd known she'd been on the train all the while.

The train pulled away, taking her farther from him and returning her to her flat, her life. She wouldn't see those eyes again. She couldn't possibly. The astronomical odds that had caused her such discomfort today couldn't possibly occur again. He was a stranger, and a stranger he would remain.

Rachel relaxed into her seat, pulled out one of the redundant headphones and wriggled her shoulder to disturb the girl beside her.

"Hey." She smiled as Andy woke. "You're cooking dinner tonight, right?"

"It's shit like this that has my sister complain that we're an old married couple." Andy stretched as she let out a yawn. "One day, Ms. Rachel King, you're going to have to learn to cook."

"But until that day, I have you." She smiled before dropping a kiss onto her forehead, choosing to ignore Andy's gentle chiding.

Andy let out a noncommittal noise and put distance between the two of them, hurriedly finding things to do: a sip of drink from her bottle, tidying away the book left forgotten as she'd slept, tying her hair with a band from her wrist.

"Ands." Rachel tried to still her.

"Don't." She was warned, Andy's dark brown eyes briefly looking up and meeting her own.

Rachel thought of the boy's. His were blue, they had flecks of brown just like her own.

Just like her own.

But that was . . .

It wasn't, but it should be.

Somewhere in the house in Epping where Rachel grew up there

was a photograph of a woman, white blouse and a yellow cardigan, she had dark hair and her eyes, shadowed by an equally dark powder, were similar. Those eyes were similar, but even they weren't the same.

His shouldn't have been.

Yet his were.

Blue, flecks of brown, just like her own.

The train was suddenly too loud. It was all she could hear. No. That wasn't true. She could hear everything. Her breathing. The blood pumping through her head. She could feel it, too. She felt cold, unnaturally so, but she also felt hot. Too hot. As if her body were trying to escape itself. She realised she was wearing her jacket still— she hadn't taken it off when she'd boarded the train. She needed it off. It was too much. It was all too much.

"Rach." Andy's hand touched hers, her fingers soft on the back of her hand; she felt the tips rubbing circles across the bones hidden beneath the thin skin. Andy's fingers were warm, somehow managing to be hotter and colder than Rachel's own body temperature.

"Rach," she repeated, "I need you to breath. Can you do that for me?"

Henry

HE HAD ALWAYS known he was adopted. It was as much a part of him as the hairs on his head, the couple of moles on his shoulder, or the slight protrusion of his belly button. He had always known he was adopted. That he was special. That he had been chosen.

Other boys and girls were born, yet he had been handpicked to be loved by his mother and father, making him the most wanted child in all the world.

Every night, after his mother read whatever book he'd chosen, she would lay him down, tuck him in and lie beside him. She would wrap an arm around him, place her head next to his, and recount how he had come into her life as he drifted to sleep beside her. Wrapped in the warmth of her arms. Wrapped in the warmth of her love.

Your father and I, before we were even married, always knew we wanted a little man in our home. I always knew he would be called Henry Alexander Cole—

Daddy wanted to call me David.

Yes, dear, he did. But your father doted on me, almost as much as he doted on you, and always let me win—

What does doted mean?

To love dearly.

As he grew, and his bedtime stories changed from Shirley Hughes to Roald Dahl, and his interruptions evolved.

Do you think you would love me more if I'd grown inside you?

15

Nothing could make me love you more.

How do you know that?

Because I can feel it in my heart.

From then on, when he laid his head down, when his mother tucked him in and lay down beside him, he would place his hand over her chest and feel her heart as she told his story. Their story. He would feel her heart and he would feel her love coursing through it.

"Why didn't you and Daddy have a baby of your own?" he asked tentatively one night, his hand resting on her chest. She was silent so long that he started to fear he'd said something bad. He opened his mouth to take it back.

"Your father was a great man." He could hear the pain in her voice. He could hear how much the words were hurting her, how hard she was trying to push away the hurt and the pain, so her words could reach him. "He was a brilliant man. He was an intelligent, talented, funny, generous man. But he was also a sad man."

He could feel her heart beating beneath his hand. So full of love. So full of pain.

"He was a sad man," his mother tried again.

"Like when I fell off the climbing frame and had to have my arm in a cast?"

She shook her head.

"Like when David Tennant had to regenerate into Matt Smith?"

She shook her head.

"Like how you are now?"

"No." He could feel her chest tightening, like every word was a battle. "He was a sad man, like adults get sad sometimes without being able to explain why. Like everything hurts but there isn't a reason."

"There's always a reason."

"No." Her voice was so quiet. "My precious, precious little man, there isn't."

That was when he had realised that some questions shouldn't be asked.

The first time he had met someone like him, the first time he _knew_ he'd met someone like him, was in a history lesson in his new school. Much like his new uniform, the school was too big for him. Out of the confines of his small village primary school, he found himself swamped by all the other children suddenly surrounding him. There were more children his age, in his year, than there had been in the entire playground of his primary school. His summer birthday meant that he was barely eleven. He focused on making new friends, meeting his new teachers, finding his place in this new school, to do as his mother advised: _turn fears into possibilities._

Yet the school still seemed much too big for him.

The first time he knew he'd met someone like him, the girl was crying. They had been asked to complete a timeline of their lives. Timelines, he was told by his new teacher, are how historians piece together the past. He liked history. History was stories that were real, history was how they came to be, history was who they were.

Romans.	Birth.
Anglo-Saxons.	Adoption.
Middle Ages.	Preschool.
Tudors.	Primary School.
Stuarts.	Secondary School.
Georgians.	History class.
Victorians.	Grace crying.
WWI & WWII.	Grace running out of history.
Now.	Now.

Grace had never been adopted though, so Grace's timeline was very different to Henry's.

Birth.
Court case.

Foster home.
Appeal.
Foster home.
Preschool.
Failed adoption.
Foster home.
Primary School.
Foster home.
Foster home.
Secondary School.
Foster home.
History class.
Crying.
Running.
Now.

Grace's timeline was a lot longer than Henry's. Grace had never been chosen. Grace had never been special. Grace had never had parents that knew her name before they'd even held her. Grace had never had a daddy that wanted to call her one name but went with another because he doted on her mummy as well as her. Grace had never been loved dearly.

From then on, he stayed out of Grace's way in school and kept his head down. He didn't want Grace reminding him of what his life could have been like, he didn't want to see what it was like for those that weren't chosen. He didn't want to know what it was like for them. He shouldn't have to know. Instead, Henry did his homework and worked hard. He wanted to be a brilliant man like his father. But also needed to be a happy man. A perfect man. A man to justify his being chosen.

But then he was leaning against the shop window in St Pancras. He was waiting for the others to return. Sam was taking them all to a football game. He was going to see Ozil, Lacazette and Aubameyang.

He was going to the Emirates for the first time.

But then he saw her.

It took him a while to place her. She hadn't been one of his primary school teachers. She wasn't the mother of one of his friends. She hadn't been one of those women that volunteered at Cubs. He knew all the people she wasn't, but couldn't work out who she *was*. But he knew he recognised her, and that the last time he'd seen her she had been much younger.

Then he found her at the back of all his memories.

The last time he'd seen her she had been in a photograph. She had been a photograph of a young girl, barely older than himself, she was scruffy and angry and pregnant. The last time he'd seen her she had been a photograph amongst his adoption papers in his mother's drawer of boring adult things. He'd walked in on his mother sat filing, bank statements or something else that didn't hold his attention, on the floor of her study. He'd seen the photograph lying on the carpet and picked it up. He'd asked his mother who the girl was and why she looked so angry. His mother wasn't able to tell him why the girl was angry, but she had explained that the girl had given birth to him.

Henry had sat down, photograph still in hand, and rested his head on his mother's legs, allowing her to stroke his hair as she told him about her. There was a blank space in his memory where a name should be. He could remember it all, the boring papers surrounding them, the feel of the old photograph in his hand and its battered edges, the gentle touch of his mother's fingers running through his hands. *She will always have a special place in my heart*, his mother continued, *for she gave me my son. The most loved little man in the world.* He could remember everything but the name of the girl in the photograph.

Henry caught the girl—a woman now—looking back at him as he waited for his mother to emerge from the toilets in St Pancras. Her face was thinner now, the hair straighter than before, but the features—the shape of her nose, the fullness of her lips, the eyes—it was unmistakable. The woman was the same girl from the photograph. Only the woman didn't look angry anymore, she just looked sad.

Isaac barrelled into his leg, chatting excitedly into his stomach. The small boy couldn't wait to see Ozil, to see Lacazette, to see *"Bangy-yang"*—he was scooped up into his father's arms before he could continue.

"Your mother still queuing?"

"Guess so." Henry shrugged and pulled out his phone, a barrier to put between Sam and himself. Something else to look at other than the woman standing across from him.

He should be excited. He should be happy. He should be perfect. He needed to be perfect, otherwise he would be like Grace, and he would be returned.

He looked back at the woman. Rachel King. That was her name.

He had been baby King before he had been passed to his mother and she held him to her chest. Then he became Henry Alexander Cole. He had been Henry Alexander Cole for so much longer than he had ever been baby King.

His mother had taken Isaac into her arms and was complaining to him about something, laughing as she did, when the woman and her friend walked passed them. Without thinking, without blinking, his arm shot out and his hand wrapped around Rachel King's arm.

"I'm sorry," Henry said quietly, looking up and meeting her eyes. Blue, flecks of brown. Stark contrast to the blonde of her hair, to the green of her jumper. Blue, flecks of brown. Like his own. "I know you."

"No." She shook her head, pulled her arm free and caught up with her friend.

"Who was that?" Sam asked.

Henry looked to his mother, searching for a sign, anything that she had seen the woman too, that she had recognised her to be Rachel King. That his mother knew the woman that would always have a special place in her heart because Rachel had given her a child—*her son.* But there was nothing there. Only what seemed to be confusion.

"What were you thinking, Henry?" His mother was scolding him. Angry even. He'd been way off when he'd guessed confusion. "You can't just grab people you see on the street. For god's sake, this is London." He was sure that it was only Isaac in her arms that stopped her from gesticulating wildly. "She could have been anyone."

"But—" She wasn't just anyone, he wanted to tell her. The words didn't come out though. He couldn't end his sentence, not even a timid protest to his mother's annoyance? Anger? Fear?

Elizabeth

SAM HAD OFFERED to take Isaac to the male toilets, so she wouldn't have to occupy the small boy while she waited in line for the lady's. She would have been grateful for the company however, as the queue was, as it always would be, long and tedious. Two were out of order, an attendant walking between the working ones fruitlessly. There was nothing to be done, nothing to be improved.

She'd had to cough behind a woman's shoulder to be able to make her way to the sink to wash her hands. The woman next to her was touching up her makeup and checked her reflection in both mirror and the camera in her phone. Apparently, she'd found an issue in what Elizabeth considered flawless Mediterranean skin, because she rummaged through her bag for concealer. Elizabeth only wanted water, soap, and to leave as quickly as possible.

Their day in London had barely begun, yet she was already stressed. There were too many people, they were everywhere, and there would only be more when they arrived at the football stadium. Sam hadn't thought this day out at all; they shouldn't have brought Isaac with them, it was going to be too much for a toddler to cope with. It was too much for her to cope with.

She looked in the mirror and watched the woman fuss with her hair before departing. When Elizabeth had been this woman's age, she'd already had Henry. She would have been rummaging for wet wipes amongst Ziploc bags of carrot sticks and raisins. Fifteen years later she found her bag had those same things in again, Sam never remembering to carry such things.

Walking back out into the main station, she found Henry on his phone, desperately trying to ignore Sam. Henry should have been excited, Sam was taking him to see Henry's beloved Arsenal play for the first time. Yet the entire journey up to London he'd sat with his headphones in, staring out the window, making himself appear as small as possible. Henry had been acting like this since she'd given Sam a key and asked him to water the plants while she and Henry had gone to Scotland for a fortnight. That was nearly three months ago. The key she'd leant Sam was now firmly attached to his others; when she'd gone to ask for it back, he'd been in her kitchen cooking her a Thai green curry, a goofy smile covering his face as he prepared the chicken, modesty hidden behind a Cath Kidston apron the question died on her lips.

The football game was Sam's treat, trying to find something, anything that would win over her son's affections. Sam was oblivious to many things, but Henry's distain to him was not one of them; he knew he needed more than the ability to cook and a cheeky smile to get Henry on board.

"Be glad you'll never have to experience women's toilets," she told Isaac as she took him into her arms. "Never enough, and always at least one out of order."

Isaac's attention was taken by Henry though, who was grabbing a woman by the arm as she passed by. The stranger turned to face them all, dropping her head quickly to avoid eye contact and hiding behind a curtain of messy blond hair.

"I know you." Henry's hand was still around her arm as he moved his head trying to find her gaze.

"No!" The woman shook herself free of him and ran to catch up with her friend.

"Who was that?" Sam asked.

"What were you thinking, Henry?" She ignored Sam and focussed her attention on her son. "You can't just grab people you see on the street. For god's sake, this is London. She could have been anyone." She could have been in a gang, had a knife, accused him of god knows what. Elizabeth continued her worries in her head; she didn't need to burden Henry with them too.

"But—"

She silenced Henry's defence with a shake of her head. She couldn't hear any more, and they needed to move on from this incident so they could enjoy the day ahead of them.

She tried to stand up straighter, rebalancing Isaac on her hip as she did so, pulling the small boy's coat tighter around him. "Come on then, let's go to this football game."

* * *

"Is that Sam's wife?"

"Ex-wife," Elizabeth corrected as they watched the three from the car.

"How old is she?"

"Early thirties."

She tried to look away, but like Henry, she was entranced by the picture before her. Isaac had run along the path to his mother as she opened the door, his tiredness forgotten in his excitement to be reunited with his mother. Sam followed behind with the superhero rucksack of supplies and a plastic carrier of souvenirs from their afternoon at the football.

"Is English her first language?"

"Henry!" She spun round in her seat so she could look at her son strapped in behind her.

"What? She's Filipino, right? I don't know what language they speak. You guys never talk about her, how am I meant to know?"

"Shocking that we don't speak about Sam's ex-wife in your presence." Elizabeth sighed and returned to face the front.

"Do you ever talk about Dad?" Henry asked quietly as Sam made his way back up the path and towards the car.

"There's nothing to say."

"But I thought he was brilliant?"

"Like you're brilliant," she tried to reassure but Sam pulled at the driver's door and Henry's attention was back to his phone.

* * *

Monday night she returned from work and found Henry in his room, and as she entered, he'd quickly flicked between programmes on his computer, hiding whatever it was he'd been doing. Mutterings about homework and food were exchanged, but then Sam was heard entering the house and Henry retreated within himself. He came downstairs and ate supper with the both of them, but returned to his room as soon as he was able, having not said a word. Elizabeth could feel him pulling away, the boy she'd raised and loved with all her heart, perhaps too much of her heart. Her love for her son was all consuming, leaving little room for others.

She'd discussed it with Caitlin, as she discussed everything with her. Caitlin had put it down to hormones, suggested that there might be a girl in Henry's life—*or a boy*, Caitlin had added quickly and almost timidly before changing the subject entirely.

Elizabeth neither knew nor cared what the issue was, she just wanted Henry to talk to her about it. Henry had never been shy about sharing things with her, more often than not he told her more than she wished to know, and frequently at the most inopportune moments, but recently he'd become quieter and quieter. She feared it had everything to do with the fact that Sam had a key to their house, that he could come and go as he pleased.

But it had been fifteen years since . . .

She deserved something of her own.

Tuesday Elizabeth came home to much the same scene: there was a textbook open by his desktop, but it was clear it wasn't homework Henry had been doing. Elizabeth simply sat on his bed, her legs tightly crossed, her hands balled in her lap, crescent moons etching themselves onto her palms. Her middle finger flicking across the tip of her thumb.

She stared at the poster in front of her as she thought about how to phrase her questions about Sam to her son. Sam was a good man, Sam loved her, Sam could love Henry too, if only he'd let him.

She stared at the poster in front of her as she thought about the only man she'd had in her life for fifteen years. It was the Arsenal team photo for the season. She busied herself trying to name all the players Henry had told her about: she recognised most of the front row, the middle was a stretch, and the only person she could name in the back row was a goalkeeper. Petr Cech. Henry had been so excited when he had signed for Arsenal. He spoke nonstop about his legacy at Chelsea: how they had betrayed him, *Courtois had nothing on him*; about his head injury and why he always wore a skull cap. He had even pulled up a meme to show her. Arsene Wenger and Cech photoshopped into *Lord of the Rings*. *Bloody Stephen Hunt, could have ended his career,* he'd practically shouted.

Henry! He had never sworn before, certainly never in front of her, that's how excited he had been. But Arsene Wenger was gone now. Henry said it was time for a new dawn at Arsenal. She wondered if the same was being applied to her own home.

Henry had never shown an interest in sport until he started school. Henry told people that his love of football came from his first day, that it hadn't been the other children he spoke about, the teachers or his classroom, it was that the bigger boys had played football with him that had been the best bit of starting school.

It was during his Year Three parents' evening, however, the first year Henry had ever had a male teacher, that it was suggested that she let him join the football team. *He's got a natural talent. If he likes it, you should think about taking him along to one of the local junior teams. My mate coaches the under nines if you're interested.*

When she'd got home, sent away the babysitter and finally slipped off her heels, she walked up to his room and found him still awake reading a comic by torchlight. She lay him down, tucked him in and laid beside him. She wrapped an arm around him, placed her head next to his and told him all about what Mr. Holt had said. That weekend they went and bought his first pair of football boots. The boy in the shop had tried to persuade them that Henry needed the same boots that Christiano Ronaldo wore. Henry wanted the boots that Adebayor wore. *Arsenal are way better than Manchester United, Mum, everyone knows that.*

She didn't know that, and she didn't know that Henry knew that. She wondered how long he had known and not told her, she wondered if he would have told his father.

Henry swivelled in his chair, bringing her attention back to him. "Mum—"

But then the front door slammed shut below them, announcing Sam's return. Henry turned back to his computer and to the homework he was pretending to be doing, whatever it was he would have said disturbed and pushed aside by Sam's return home.

"Elizabeth? Henry?" Sam called softly up the stairs, his loud actions always making up for the quietness of his voice.

"You'd better go," Henry told her. "Sam's here."

"He can wait." Elizabeth opened her mouth to say more, for she had so much to say to him. She wanted to pull him close to her, but she could see Henry rallying against her.

"No, he can't." Henry's words were slow and deliberate, as if he had been rehearsing them, practicing this argument in his head and he was only now ready to have it. "He lives here now. You should go see to him."

"He doesn't live here," she said quickly, straightening her skirt as she stood.

"Feels like it." Henry had spun back around in his chair, his back to her and a video game screen loading.

"He's a good man." She'd tried, a hand reaching out to touch him. "He makes me smile."

"No, he doesn't." And that closed the conversation. Henry had put headphones in and shut her out again.

Elizabeth had gone downstairs to find Sam arranging flowers in a vase. *Not nearly as pretty as you though*, he'd told her as he trimmed the bottoms. She'd kissed him on the cheek and pulled his arms around her, his embrace so warming after the coldness of upstairs. Henry was right about a good many things, but this he was wrong about. Sam did make her smile.

It was Wednesday now. Wednesdays she got home first where Henry had football practice. He was getting so good. *The complete midfielder*, she'd been told last time she'd spoken with his coach. She didn't know what that meant, she doubted his father would have known either. Sam spoke about watching Henry play at one of his games, he'd shared the view that Henry was a complete midfielder from the bits he'd seen of Henry play in the park or the garden. She hadn't asked him what that meant. She didn't want it to be Sam that told her, she wanted it to be Henry. He used to tell her everything, whether she wanted to know or not. She wanted to return to that.

Glancing at the clock in the corner of her computer, she started to pack up her things for the day. She'd pop to Tesco on the way home and pick up something nice to cook for supper. Henry would be famished after his football practice. She would send a text to Sam, make sure he spent the night at his, and she would ask Henry what a complete midfielder was, and she would keep asking questions until Henry spoke again, to bring her son back to her, to return to the way things were and how they should be.

Rachel

SHE WAS MAKING coffee in the flat, the cat dancing between her legs and purring gently as she prepared the cafetière. She had beaten Andy home from work, as she did most nights, and so it fell to her to start the coffee and ready the TV; they would watch a quiz show before dinner as they did most nights. The cat fussed around her, obviously happy to have company again.

The kettle boiled as the buzzer rang; she looked between the two before turning to the cat. "Your human has forgotten her keys again," she complained as she made her way to the intercom. She unlocked the communal door two floors below without bothering to glance at the grainy image of the person on the doorstep.

She was able to look through the cupboards, the fridge, and the freezer and deem that they needed to go shopping again if they were going to eat that evening before the knock came on the door.

"Ands!" She headed in her direction. "Tell me you stopped at Asda, tell me that you're a good provider, and that I'll never find a woman as good as you." She was laughing as she opened the door, but that laughter quickly died.

He was wearing his thick winter coat again. It fitted him better today, with all the various layers of his school uniform beneath it.

The coldness she'd felt on the train returned, it started in her shoulders and ran down her back like water in a shower, the iciness of fear tickling down until it puddled around her feet. It weighed down her tongue and made it impossible to speak.

The teenager pulled out a folded piece of paper from his blazer pocket, silently ironing out the creases before reading from it: "You're Rachel King. Born fifteenth February 1985. Colchester General Hospital, Essex." He looked up, unsure if he should continue.

She shook her head. She needed to just shut the door, put a barrier between the boy and herself. Force him out and away. She couldn't do this.

Her head shook again, as if adamant that it would be enough to dampen his curiosity, if not extinguish it completely. That disappointment could push him away.

But Andy was walking up the stairs, calling out to her.

"What would you do without me, Rach?" She was smiling as she ascended the last stair, flicking through the mail.

Rachel closed her eyes and tried to swallow the taste of fear in her mouth. She opened them again when she felt the cat at her legs demanding release into the hall. Scooping him up into her arms, she looked back at the landing. The scene was no different: Andy was still smiling obliviously, and the teenager was still staring at her, waiting for her lie to end.

"I'll tell you what you'd do"— Andy continued as if she came home to this gathering every evening, pushing passed the teenager, unperturbed by his presence —"you'd never check the post and thus never pay your credit card bill and be destitute and alone, that's what you'd do without me."

She deposited the letters on the small table by the door, dropped her bag and shrugged off her coat. "You going to tell me who the kid is, or do I have to wait for Pete to learn English?" she asked, taking the cat into her own arms.

"Doesn't matter, the kid can't stay."

"Okay," she drawled out. "Come on, Pete, let's go and find come coffee."

As soon as Andy's back was turned, a young hand snatched out and grabbed the post that had been brought in. Rachel cursed herself for not being faster.

"Rachel King," the boy read out, riffling through them. "R. King. Miss R. King. Rachel King."

She rolled her tongue around her mouth and her teeth bit down timidly on her lower lip.

"You're not her?" the boy questioned incredulously, placing the envelopes back on the small table with the rest of her unopened mail.

"I'm not who you want me to be," she rephrased.

"Who do I want you to be?"

The arch of his eyebrow transported her back to her A Level English class. Daniel was challenging the teacher, refusing to believe whatever interpretation he had just delivered. In a minute the teenager on her doorstep would run his fingers through the slight cowlick in his auburn hair and the two boys would be indistinguishable.

Except for the eyes, blue with flecks of brown. Just like her own.

"Your mother."

Silence.

Henry remained in the hallway, one hand wrapped around the strap of his school bag, keeping it in place on his shoulder, the other holding the piece of paper he had produced from his pocket. That hand was shaking. Had Rachel removed her second hand from her pocket, he would have seen that hers was shaking too.

She needed to say something, but if she opened her mouth she'd take in water. It would pull her down. There would be no escape. No, what she needed was for *him* to say something. Anything. To yell. To cry. Yet he simply stood there, putting the onus on her to react, to take the lead, to be the adult, the parent.

What would she have done if the situation were reversed? She'd imagined it, of course she had. But in her mind, her parents would reach out to her, to find her, to make amends.

Andy was in the kitchen talking to Pete.

She could hear her heart's desperate rhythm. She could hear the words left unsaid.

She heard everything and nothing at all.

Andy popped around the corner, holding Pete close to her chest, and Rachel felt her watching them, clearly wondering which one of them would crack first.

"Can you either invite him in or shut the door? Pete isn't going to want to be held forever."

"The kid can't stay." A sentence Rachel hoped would convince the boy leave, turn around and forget whatever intentions had brought him to her doorstep. Whatever the boy wanted or needed from her, she would be unable to provide. A fact that had remained constant in the boy's sixteen years.

"I'm not leaving."

Rachel looked towards him and spotted the same mask of resolution she'd often worn herself as a teenager.

"Look—"

"Do we have a problem?" Andy brushed past them and shoved Pete behind the first door she could reach. "Do I need to call the police?" Pete's clawing at the door he was locked behind was her only answer.

Rachel pulled her eyes away from the boy in front of her and found Andy ducked down on the floor, rummaging through her handbag, obviously looking for her mobile. Rachel resigned herself to the outcome of the evening and released the door from her grasp.

"Don't bother," she told her, stepping out of the doorway and heading towards the sofa. "They'll take his side."

"His side?" Andy questioned, abandoning her search and crouching down before her. Rachel sent a quick glance to the boy still in the hallway, and Andy's eyes followed the movement. "Rach, are you in trouble?" She grabbed her knee, squeezing it between her fingers. They were still warm from where she'd been holding the cat for so long. "What have you done?"

"She hasn't done anything." The teenager was quietly standing in front of them, shooting anxious glances between the two.

The front door was shut yet Pete still clawed at the bathroom door detaining him. Rachel would have done the same. She just wanted to be let out. She was suffocating in the close confines of her flat.

"He's my son," she said quietly, realising there was no other option, no other way that this would end.

The tightness around her chest didn't lessen any with the admission; if anything, the air got thicker in the room, and she was choking on it.

Andy studied her, then turned to the boy. Her mouth opened and closed as questions were seemingly phrased and rephrased.

Rachel didn't wait to hear any of them. She couldn't process Henry's presence in her home herself, let alone handhold someone else through the discovery of her childhood pregnancy.

Her palm pressed against her chest and she was on her feet, Andy struggled to maintain her balance, but Rachel didn't care. She needed to be anywhere but there. She pushed passed the teenager and locked herself behind the bathroom door.

She pressed her back against the door and slid to the floor, pushing her palms onto the cold tiles, trying to regain control of her breathing.

Five things you can see: toilet, shower, sink, hamper, towels.

Four things you can hear: dripping, Pete, talking—

She pulled off her socks and pulled up her trouser legs as far as they would go up her calves. She then pushed her legs down onto the cold of the tiles and replaced her hands either side of her hips.

Five things you can see: toilet in the corner, needs a new seat; shower next to it; sink opposite, hot tap still leaking; washing hamper that Pete's been sleeping in; towels I dropped on the floor, equally covered in cat hair.

Four things you can hear: that damned dripping tap; Pete

purring, kneading away at the towels on the floor; Andy talking to the kid—

She swallowed the sharp taste of bile flooding her mouth and rearranged her body so as much of her could be touching the cold floor as possible. She took a deep breath and forced herself forward.

Andy talking to my son in the next room; the dancing of the solar powered Hula Girl on the window sill.

Three things you can feel: the coldness of the floor tiles; the wooden panels of the door against my back; Pete rubbing himself against my exposed leg.

Two things you can smell or taste: that wretched reed infuser Andy insisted on buying; that acidic taste that comes with blind, unwavering panic.

One deep breath in through your mouth. Hold it. Slowly release through your nose.

One deep breath in through yo—

The knock against the door rattled against her back.

"It's only me," Andy whispered through it. Rachel let go of the floor and reached above her head. She unlocked the door from where she sat and pushed herself away from it so she was pressed to the wall opposite. Andy slowly entered and joined her on the floor. "Henry is in my room, watching TV whilst we figure out what to do."

"Henry." She nodded, remembering the letters her social worker had showed her. His name was Henry. Henry Alexander Cole. Henry after the woman's father. Alexander after the boy's own.

Andy's hand snaked out and grabbed hers. It was so warm.

They simply sat there. Backs against the wall. Hands held. Pete winding himself through their legs.

"I was barely seventeen," Rachel told her eventually. "Lower sixth, when I discovered I was pregnant. I dropped out. Had him. Put him up for adoption."

The words were running away from her, she was chasing after them, but her legs weren't in control. Step after step after step. If she stopped, she would fall and she didn't think she would be able to get back up, the words would be out of sight, never to be seen again. There was no other option, she had to keep up the chase.

"Found a family for him. Pretended it never happened. Went to college. Got my A Levels. Went to university. Went to a *different* university—"

"Met me."

Her hand was squeezed between hers. She could tell Andy was trying to slow her down, to get her to breathe, but if she slowed down, if she took breath, she wouldn't be able to tell her. She would stop, she would fall, and the words would be gone forever.

"Met you." Rachel nodded. "Graduated. Followed you around Europe. Sixteen years later he sees me at a train station. He hunts me down. Knocks on my door. I have a panic attack and lock myself in the bathroom."

"The teenager that grabbed you." Andy's voice was soft, it kept her in grounded, tethering her to the earth yet she so desperately wanted to be allowed to drift off.

"The teenager that grabbed me." She was nodding again. "Luke was banging on at me down the phone. Something about the museum or the children. I don't know. I wasn't listening." She shook her head and pushed away her procrastination. "I saw the kid leaning against one of the shop windows. He was staring at me with such a level of concentration that I felt like he was trying to see into my soul. It wasn't until he got off the train at Ashford I realised why. I should have seen it earlier, he looks just like his father did at his age."

"Who—"

"Boy in school," Rachel finished for her flatly. "Not to sound too *Harry Potter*, but he has my eyes." Rachel looked across at her best friend and smiled weakly. The smile that Andy returned with didn't reach her eyes.

"You need to talk to him. To Henry," she clarified.

"I know." Rachel sighed. "I'd rather stay in here."

"I know." Andy went to stand up, a struggle, as she refused to release Rachel's hand. "I can—"

"No." She shook her head as she allowed Andy to pull her to her feet. "I should probably do this alone."

"Or you could do it in the kitchen, sit at the table, and I could potter around you both. Make dinner. Pretend I'm neither there nor listening."

Rachel shrugged.

Andy pulled her close and held her tighter than she'd ever been held before. Her hand was at the back of her head and she held her like Rachel was child.

"I love you," she whispered into her hair.

"Love you too." Rachel nodded into her shoulder.

"I would make you a wonderful wife if, you know . . ."

"This is what I've been trying to tell you for years." Rachel didn't realise she was crying until she felt Andy's wet hair against her cheek. Andy simply held her tighter, trying in vain to contain her shaking body as it admitted silent sobs.

She pushed herself up and away, and at the sink she splashed her face with cold water. When she looked up, she found Andy watching her in the mirror.

* * *

They sat at opposite sides of the small table that separated the kitchen from the rest of the living room. Her hands were wrapped around her coffee cup; he had tea in front of him but hadn't touched it as he had been too busy going through printouts about her life. The question of how he'd managed to find her had been made redundant by the various pieces of social media laid out between them.

"If you don't want people to find you, you should change your privacy settings. I could show you how, if you want." There was a shrug as he brought a print screen of an old Myspace page to the top. "You should probably stop checking in at places whenever you go somewhere at the very least."

Andy had anglicised her name for Facebook—swapped Grigoriadis for Gregory when she'd started her teacher training—Rachel had mocked her for it at the time. *Who's going to stalk you on Facebook?* She now wondered what name she could have put instead. Thoughts went to a child's football shirt in a box beneath her bed–*Milner 9*–the white with the blue trim of that season's Spurs kit, never worn but loved all the same.

"Where do your mum and dad think you are?" She placed her LinkedIn profile over the rest of her digital footprint. It needed updating. She should probably think about looking for a new job soon, Brexit was slowly ruining her current one.

He bristled before her. "My *mum*," he emphasised a little too forcefully, "thinks I'm at football practice."

"When should you be home?"

He looked around the room for the time. "Now?"

She sipped from her coffee and ran her fingers through her hair before tying into a messy bun using a band from her wrist.

"You okay getting back to the sta—"

"Rachel!" The pair of them looked at Andy who was still pretending to be making dinner, even though it was obvious she'd finished a while ago. "A word?"

She looked back to the boy at the table, before standing up and following Andy into her bedroom. She sat down beside Pete curled up by one of Andy's pillows and automatically started stroking his head. He let out a disgruntled yawn at being disturbed, rearranged himself and pushed his head into her hand asking for more.

"You can't let Henry travel back by himself."

"Why not?"

"For fuck's sake, Rach—"

"Don't treat me like one of your pupils."

"Don't act like one then!" Rachel could see Andy's frustration with her building, but she didn't know what she'd done to trigger it. All she'd done was ask Henry if he could get back okay. "He lied to his mum about coming here. What's to stop him lying to *you* about returning?"

"Neither of us has a car." Rachel held her hands out, her palms upwards, almost waiting for a solution to fall into them. "We can't drive him home."

"You'll have to call his mum, she'll have to come and get him."

Rachel quickly retracted her hands and wrapped her arms across herself, hoping her actions had been quick enough to hide her discomfort from Andy.

"What am I meant to say? 'Hi, the kid I gave you is here, and I want you to take him back?'"

Henry stepped into the room and passed her his phone, his mother's number ready for her to call. She squeezed her thumb tightly between her fingers before accepting the mobile. "Just tell her your postcode and she'll come get me."

"You don't think I should say anything else?" Rachel looked between the two stood above her.

Neither answered.

Henry merely took his lip between his teeth, shook his head and walked back out into the living room. Andy gave her shoulder a squeeze before following him out.

Rachel heard Andy say something about putting the TV on as she stared at the phone in her hand. The screen displayed three numbers: Home, Mobile, Work all under the banner of Mum.

There was a photo to go with her name—a picture of her holding him close as he held the camera at an awkward angle to take a selfie. He looked like he was taller than her. He looked happy, so did his mother.

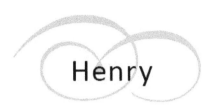

Henry

ANDREA FOLLOWED HENRY back out into the living room. He was tidying the collection of papers still scattered on the table, sorting them back into chronological order, back into their folder.

Henry had applied the same level of thoroughness to researching his birth mother as he put into his school work. As if it were coursework for his GCSEs, as if he would receive a mark or a qualification afterwards. He was in the first year of his A Levels now; the coursework was a lot harder, so his research had to be more thorough.

He had started with Google. He had found her Facebook page, her face beaming on the screen, separating her from all the other Rachel Kings listed and, from the expansive details she'd posted, he was able to glean more and more information. It always surprised him how much adults complained about internet safety and yet seemed willing to upload their whole lives to it: no wonder his mum was so frightened by it.

This Rachel King—*his Rachel King*—worked in an office, something to do with boats and shipping. Half of the information about the company was in French. He couldn't work out what the company did exactly, he just knew that it was Belgian but had offices in Dover.

Finding her actual address had been surprisingly easily. Every time she'd uploaded a picture, there was a small map with a red dot dropped onto it. She seemed to check in every time she went somewhere or uploaded a new photograph. When he'd first seen her, she had been on her way to the Science Museum, then she'd gone to Pizza Express for something to eat. She had checked in each time.

All her pictures were tagged. He found out the name of the woman she'd been in London with. She'd gone with Andrea Gregory, a Luke and an Imogen Milner had been there too, along with a boy and a girl. He found pictures of her and Andrea in pubs, usually The Hanging Man.

They checked in whenever they went. He found pictures of her at parties, pinpointing her to locations in Southend, Canterbury, and Deal. Then he found a picture of a party she had thrown in Dover, where she lived with Andrea, marking them to their home, their faces beaming, a small sentence bragging about the amount of noise they were about to make at their housewarming.

"Sit," Andrea commanded, pointing to the chair nearest his cold cup of tea before going to the kitchenette. She flicked about with the stove, reheating whatever it was she had cooked before.

"What do you do?" he asked, watching her start to grate some hard cheese into a bowl. "I couldn't see your job on your Facebook profile."

"That's not creepy at all." She turned around to face him, she was smiling as she scolded him. "I'm a reception class teacher."

"In Dover?"

She nodded as she placed the bowl of cheese in front of him.

"How about you? Where do you go to school?"

Henry was suddenly conscious of the uniform he was wearing. "Ashford," he replied, nervously tugging at his blazer.

"GCSEs?"

"A Levels now."

"Enjoying it?"

Andrea put a plate of food in front of him; both the question she'd asked and any answer he could come up with forgotten. She'd made pasta and a sauce from scratch. It was like his mother's bolognese, but there wasn't any beef in it.

She sat down opposite him with a plate of her own and offered him the bowl of parmesan. He waved it away, but she covered her meal with a generous helping. It looked to him as though she was eating cheese with a pasta accompaniment rather than the other way around.

"You shouldn't eat that if you're vegetarian."

She looked at him quizzically before putting a forkful in her mouth and smacking her lips.

"Mum says they use animal rennet to make it."

"It's vegan."

"You're vegan?"

Andrea nodded her head as she continued to eat her meal.

"Is Rachel?"

"No, but if she ever wants to eat, she'll eat what she's given." Andrea looked up at him and smiled across the table. "She can't cook," she explained once her mouthful had been swallowed.

They fell into silence.

"How long have you been together?"

Suddenly Andrea choking on her pasta. He instantly felt guilty for asking the question.

"I shouldn't have asked that, that was rude, wasn't it?" He looked down at the fork he was holding in his right hand. It was a habit his mum hated, that he ate with the wrong hand when he wasn't using a knife, but one she hadn't been able to break.

"Not rude, just unexpected," she clarified as she wiped her top free of pasta sauce.

"But Rachel is a lesbian, isn't she?"

"Yes."

"Is that why she didn't want me? Because she's a lesbian?"

"Jesus, Hen, talk about shooting from the hip."

There were some things Henry wasn't very good at, his mum

always complained that he couldn't read faces, but Andrea's face he knew to be panicking. He'd seen that face a lot on people, he'd started to recognise it. He'd last seen it on Caitlin when he'd asked her if she was worried about Matt sleeping with other women whilst away with work. Caitlin always made a buzzer sound when he asked her questions like that, questions she didn't want to answer, let alone think about.

Andy wasn't going to make a noise though. She didn't know she could do that.

"What?" He frowned.

"You can't just ask something like that! I didn't know you even existed yesterday. I can't even begin to hypothesise if Rach's lesbianism is the reason she gave you up."

He watched as she poked at her pasta, not eating, just pushing it around the plate.

"You're not a lesbian though." This wasn't a question, it didn't need to be.

She shrugged.

He didn't understand that response. Either she was or she wasn't.

His mum had explained to him about shades of grey, a conversation he'd failed to suppress his laughter throughout. *That book has ruined a perfectly good phrase* his mother had complained. In the end she had used Schrödinger's cat to try and explain it to him. But that didn't make any more sense. The cat was either dead or alive, just because Schrödinger didn't know couldn't change the absoluteness of it all.

He continued to watch Andrea not eat the meal in front of her, watch her look around the room for some kind of escape from his constant probing, and he thought about her interactions he'd seen of her with Rachel.

They would be together if Andrea—*Andy*—was a lesbian too, he thought. But if Andy wasn't a lesbian, why didn't she have a husband? Both women looked too old to be alone. People got married. Lesbians could get married too now. Matt had come home from work and spoken at length about it, Caitlin had simply rolled her eyes. Henry had even made posters about it for his citizenship class. His mum had helped him. His poster had a print out of Elton John. They'd sung songs from *The Lion King* as they stuck everything onto the A3 piece of paper.

Elton John wasn't his real name. He was Reginald Kenneth Dwight. Henry wondered if he had been Elton Hercules John longer than he had been Reginald Kenneth Dwight, like he had been Henry Alexander Cole longer than he had been baby King. He wondered which name was on Elton's marriage certificate. Henry suddenly didn't know which name would be on his.

Elizabeth

SHE WAS DRIVING when the call came through. Her car told her that it was Henry on the phone, triggering a smile as she pushed the connection button on her steering wheel.

"I'm just turning into the village now," she answered the call. Henry didn't reply. He was calling, so why was he not speaking to her?

"Henry?"

"It's, uh, it's not Henry," a woman's voice said.

She pulled the car over and switched on her hazard lights. She snatched up her phone from the cup holder. Her heart was beating at such a rate she didn't know how her chest was able to contain it. There was a stranger on the end of her son's phone without explanation, she would not be having a conversation with them over speaker phone, she would not be having this conversation through her steering wheel.

"Why do you have my son's mobile?" she asked, the phone pressed so tightly to her ear that she could feel the back of her earring pinching her skin.

"He's, uh—"

"Where is my son?" Elizabeth snapped.

"He's in my flat in Dover."

She couldn't feel her heart any more, in fact she couldn't feel anything.

"He came to find me."

"Who the hell are you?"

The woman on the other end of the line took a deep breath. "I'm, uh—"

"Who. Are. You?" she spoke slowly and deliberately.

"Rachel King. I'm Rachel King."

That was the moment it hit her, and Elizabeth suddenly felt everything. Every hair on her body, every pulse point, every muscle tense in her body. Her head was in a vice which tightened with every breath.

Henry Alexander Cole has two mothers.

He wasn't even speaking to her, but he was in *her* house. But that mother didn't want him, that mother had given him away, that mother had given him to her. She wanted him so much. He was the most wanted child in all the world.

"He said that if I give you my postcode, you'll come get him."

Her left hand was pulling at her hair, her right still pushing her phone into her ear. She could feel the back of her earring pinching her skin.

"How did he find you?" she managed eventually. I haven't had your address for years. You didn't want to know him. You didn't want him. You gave him away. You gave him to me. I want him.

"Evidently I need to alter my privacy settings on my Facebook." She sounded so timid, as if the child that had given away her to a stranger nearly seventeen years ago had yet to grow up. "He said he'll show me how to do it."

"He's always been good with computers."

Elizabeth spoke in the same tone she used to the other parents at Henry's football games, as if they were making polite conversation to fill the time.

"He got an 8 in his GCSE."

The autumn evening was darkening around her and she was still parked awkwardly on the side of the road on the outskirts of her village, hazard lights flashing. She was still on the phone with her son's birth mother, though neither of them were saying anything.

"So, my postcode . . ."

It would be completely dark soon, she should be home by now, cooking supper and telling Henry to take a shower before eating.

"Do you have a pen?"

Elizabeth found herself looking around her car. She reached for her handbag, realising that she had nothing to write on.

"Hold on."

She had a pack of tissues somewhere then found a pencil, a tiny one from her last trip to Argos. She scribbled on one of the tissues, but she couldn't get it to work. Suddenly it was flying through the air and hitting the passenger side window.

"You still there?"

"The pencil won't work." Her left hand continued to pull at her hair.

"Why don't I just use the kid's—"

"Henry." Elizabeth managed to breathe out through her teeth. "His name is Henry."

". . . phone and text it to you."

"Okay."

She ended the call and flung the phone down on the seat, watching it bounce off the chair and land in the foot well beside her handbag. Her hand was out of her hair and she was squeezing her thumb tightly in her fingers. Her knuckles were white, her thumb felt like it was breaking, yet she did not loosen her grip.

The last time she felt like this she had been speaking to a police officer. Henry had been only eight months old.

* * *

Elizabeth looked around, not knowing what to expect. The street looked nice, there was a little rubbish, but the street lights were all lit, the shops looked well cared for and the houses seemed clean.

Not at all like the grubby little port town portrayed on the news; there weren't migrants hopping out of lorries in the street, there wasn't the English Defence League marching to stop them. It was just a town on the tip of the country. Just a town that contained her son's birth mother.

It never occurred to her that he had grown up with the absence of three parents, she thought it was just his father he'd missed; it never occurred to her that his biological parents left a hole in his heart, too. She thought her love alone could plug the gap. It never occurred to her that her love wouldn't be enough.

He'd never asked about his birth mother, only about the mechanics of adoption, a girl in his class triggering questions she'd prepared the answers for years before. Sentences constructed of words such as *open* and *adoption,* of *UK* and *law.* Yet here she was, opposite Rachel King's flat, about to ask for her son back. She'd never prepared for this moment. How could she? Sixteen years, three months, and twenty-one days later she had to ask the woman to give up her child again. She thought taking a child from this woman—Rachel King—would only happen once.

Alex wasn't here to hold her hand this time. This time she had to do it alone. There was no preparing for this moment.

She took her phone out of the cup holder and opened up the message from her son's number—from her son's birth mother—it had the full address and instructions of how to get in.

She stepped out of her car, straightened her skirt and ironed out the crinkles in her blouse with her hands, rearranged her coat, buttoning it closed, and fiddled with her scarf. She checked her makeup one final time in her wing mirror. Then she stopped stalling, locked her car and stepped across the street to the converted town house that contained Rachel King's flat.

She followed the instructions on her phone. Walk down the side of the building. Press flat six. Wait for the door to click. Top floor. On your right.

She could hear talking from the other side of the door, three voices, another female within the flat. She rearranged her coat and scarf again, tucked her handbag in tightly under her shoulder and knocked on the door.

She heard one of them remind the other to check where Pete was and then suddenly the door opened.

Suddenly, it would always be suddenly, she was staring into the face of the woman Henry had reached out to in St Pancras. He'd known her then. Elizabeth supposed only denial had stopped her from recognising Rachel King that day, too.

Slowly the woman looked up and met her eyes.

Blue, flecks of brown, like her son's. Like their son's.

Only Rachel King's eyes looked tired, looked scared, looked powerless.

Elizabeth swallowed back all her feelings, sent her emotions down to the depths of her bones and prayed for them to stay there. This wasn't a time for feeling.

"I'm so sorry for the interruption, Ms. King." She tucked her handbag in tighter still under her shoulder. "Henry knows not to behave like this. It won't happen again."

Rachel King stepped aside and Elizabeth saw a woman, that same woman who'd managed to find fault in flawless Mediterranean skin that wretched day in London, holding a cat—presumably Pete.

And then her eyes fell onto her son, but he would not return her gaze. At this moment she was grateful, she didn't think she could cope with two sets of blue eyes, both with flecks of brown, looking at her.

"Do you want to come in?" The Mediterranean woman threw the cat behind a door and busied herself with the kettle. "We have tea, coffee . . . I didn't know how long you'd be, Henry didn't say where you were driving from, so I gave him some pasta. I hope you don't mind."

Elizabeth was still standing in the communal space of the

converted town house; Rachel King, the woman who'd given her child to a stranger and trusted them to love it, was before her, her son—their son?—still not meeting her eyes.

"Henry, say thank you to . . ."

"Andy." The other woman called out her name above the sound of the boiling kettle.

"Say thank you to Andy for supper and collect your things. We need to be going. It's a school night. You have homework to do."

She watched Henry jump to his feet as diligently as always, ever keen to please her. His coat and bag were on in an instant and he was by the door next to Rachel King, next to his birth mother who'd entrusted another to love him better.

Both their eyes suddenly locked on to hers, looked at her as if they were worried they'd disappointed her. Both sets of eyes looked so despondent.

Blue, flecks of brown.

Suddenly neither was looking at her. Henry was holding out a folder to Rachel King, presented just like a piece of his GCSE coursework. Everything was falling into place, the two nights he'd looked himself away in his bedroom, sat behind his computer, had all been building towards this. Perhaps those sixteen years, three months, and twenty-one days had all be a precursor to this moment. Henry had always been searching for one of his absent parents.

"Do you want to keep it?" he asked her.

"Do I want to keep information you found about me on the internet?"

One of Rachel King's eyebrows arched and she looked to be stifling a smirk in the same way Henry often looked when she'd said something wrong. *Nobody likes Jar Jar Binks, Mum, he almost ruined the franchise.*

Elizabeth watched her son drop his head; he looked embarrassed.

"I thought you might like it." His voice was so quiet. Elizabeth caught Rachel subconsciously bending down to hear each word. "I went on one of those genealogy websites and I was able to do a family tree—"

"I—"

"It was quite easy really; your dad was in the army. Your parents were married. There's a tonne of legal documents. It was all online."

Elizabeth watched the woman tentatively reach out and take the folder from him, as if unsure if its contents wouldn't bite.

"You found my parents?"

Rachel

THE BOY HAD confidence in his tone again, she could hear it; he was suddenly so animated, talking with his whole body. She couldn't tell who he was excitedly reeling out the information for; the fact he sounded so proud, so desperate to please, she thought it was more for his mother than for her.

"There's all these sites online, this one had a free trial." He was splitting his attention between each of them. "Don't worry Mum, I didn't steal your credit card."

Andy had stopped fussing about the kitchen, and instead her hand was rubbing circles on Rachel's back, soothing words were being whispered into her ear as Henry kept going.

"It's all there, your dad was in the army and your parents were married. There's such a paper trail, you wouldn't believe." This was the most relaxed he'd been, the most relaxed she'd seen him, even on the train, when he didn't know she was watching him. He was chatting with so much enthusiasm about what he had found, the website he had used, all the work he'd put in as if he were telling her how he'd gotten an A for his homework. "He died whilst your mum was pregnant, some kind of nail bomb in Northern Ireland." His head snapped back towards his mother. "I had no idea how bad it was— like I'd heard stuff about the IRA—but this was crazy." Then he was back looking at her. "I think your mum . . ." A shrug of his shoulders. "You were with her for a bit—"

Then just as suddenly, he stopped. His face fell and he turned back directly to his mother. Rachel could see the realisation hit him, as she'd seen it hit so many before him. The thing he hadn't explained to her yet. The one thing that everyone in the room knew except for its eldest guest.

"Rachel grew up in care. Her mum gave her up, too."

His mother fidgeted on the spot. Her face was a mask, but her discomfort was obvious. She looked up suddenly and met her gaze. Rachel could tell what was behind her eyes. Most people looked at her with pity—*It must have been so horrible for you to grow up in care*—Henry's mother didn't have that look though. It was akin to askance. Disappointment that Rachel already had another thing in common with her son, another thing that she could never share with her adopted son. Anger even.

"Say goodnight to Mrs. King. Thank her wife—"

"Andy's not her wife. Andy's straight," Henry told her quickly.

"Thank Ms.—"

"Ms. Gregory. I saw her Facebook page too. None of Rachel's friends have very good privacy settings."

"Thank Ms. Gregory for supper and say goodnight. We need to be going. We've taken up enough of their time for one evening."

"Can I see her again?"

"If Ms. King is agreeable to it."

Rachel's head looked up from the pages in her hand. She had been letting the conversation between a mother and her son happen around her; it didn't really involve her at all. She had just been staring at the small folder in her hand which was so light.

Judi had always told Rachel off for procrastinating—*never put off until tomorrow what you can do today*. Andy described her as a chronic avoider; chores, conflict, growing up.

This was one of those things she'd never done. Had never wanted to do. Yet here it was in her hand, the story of her parents. The hows, and possibly the whys, of the reason she'd been raised by Judi and Rob instead of a mum and a dad.

The small folder was so light.

"Can I?"

"Can you?" Rachel had no idea what he was asking.

"Can I see you again?"

Rachel looked to his mother, but she couldn't read her expression, so Rachel didn't know what her response should be.

"Sure," she agreed with a slight shrug.

His mother was fishing around in her handbag, pulling out a diary, a makeup bag, a packet of tissues, her purse, and then eventually a business card. Elizabeth, his mother's name was Elizabeth Cole, the small rectangle told her.

"If you contact me, we'll arrange a time. I think it would be better if you come over to ours next time."

"Sure."

"Okay. Well, goodnight Ms. King. Goodnight Ms. Gregory, and thank you for feeding my son."

"It's not actually Gregory, that's . . . you know what . . ." Andy waved away whatever she was going to say about her name. The mother didn't care, she had already turned to her son, straightening his coat and patting a palm against his cheek.

"I'll be waiting downstairs." She placed one hand on his right cheek and fussed with his coat with the other in an attempt to pull it closer around him. "I expect you there in no more than five minutes."

"Okay." They watched his mother go down the stairs, a furtive look over her shoulder back to them, before Henry turned his attention firmly to the flat. "Thank you for dinner, Andy."

"No problem, Henry, I always cook too much."

"I'll see you soon?"

He was speaking to her now. Rachel pulled her eyes from the folder again. "Sure."

"You'll talk to my mum?"

"Sure."

"You promise?"

"I promise."

With that he bounded down the stairs.

Rachel could hear the door to the street open and close behind them, hustling them out into the night. She shut her own front door and slid down it, landing on the welcome mat she'd bought with Andy from IKEA. Henry's folder of her life was still grasped tightly in her hands, his mother's business card with it.

Andy released Pete from her bedroom and joined her on the floor; Rachel's head fell against her shoulder and they simply sat there, engulfed in the silence of their small two-bedroom flat.

"What do you want to do?" Andy asked eventually.

Rachel shrugged. "Give me options."

"You could do nothing."

Rachel shook her head. "Promised the kid," she mumbled in reply. "Next."

"We could talk about it."

She could feel Andy tense as she waited for a reply, but Rachel offered her none.

"You could look through the folder in your room. *We* could look through the folder in the living room."

She noticed Andy counting out the options on her fingers, a habit she'd had since university. Rachel assumed the habit had formed long before they met.

"We could get drunk." Andy's little finger joined the others on her left hand that had risen before it.

"I like that option."

"I know you do, sweetie." There was a chaste kiss to the top of her head.

"What choice would you make?"

"You know what I'd do."

"Okay." Rachel lifted herself from Andy's shoulder and patted her knees, readying herself for standing, and offered her hand out to her friend. "There should be wine then. Tell me there's wine."

"There's always wine." Andy smiled at her, grasping the proffered hand as she stood.

Rachel allowed herself to be led to the sofa, to be pushed down and to have the throw placed over and tucked around her as if she were ill. She watched as Andy gathered the dishes, ran them under warm water and left them for the better prospect of the wine.

She placed a bottle of Merlot and two glasses on the coffee table, mirrored Rachel's position (back to the arm, knees up, feet meeting in the middle), took half the blanket and poured them each a glass of wine.

It had always been so easy with Andy, ever since she'd met her in the student union bar. Andy was living in halls, bright-eyed, bushy-tailed, eighteen years old and straight from school. Rachel was repeating a couple of years at the behest of her social worker: she'd wanted to stick with her third but allowed herself to be persuaded to transfer universities and try again. *Maybe less drinking this time.* A girl Andy was partying with had spilt her beer over Rachel as she stumbled into the toilets, one hand urgently covering her mouth. Andy had been profusely embarrassed and Rachel helped her take the girl home before anything worse could happen.

That first Christmas, after Andy had convinced her to 'blow off' Epping, she had taken her back to Ipswich to spend the break with Andy's family and friends rather than her own. New Year's Eve they had slept together. Andy had pulled her into her arms, their sweaty bodies moulding into one, and placed a tender kiss on her forehead before looking across to her, seriousness marring her nineteen-year-old features.

Jesse said he loved me before we left, Andy had whispered into her hair before getting up and leaving her for the shower.

Rachel took her glass from Andy, and then she took hers as well, placing them both back on the coffee table. She rearranged their bodies so her feet were on the ground and Andy's legs were draped across her lap. Then she kissed her. She took her lips between her own and slowly ran her tongue against them, Andy leaned in, placed one cool palm on her cheek, yet the other pushed against her chest.

"Don't do this," she responded sadly. "Your son just turned up on our doorstep, eaten dinner with us and handed you the keys to finding your own birth parents. You're not kissing me to kiss me."

"Why are you kissing me then?"

"Because you're confused."

Rachel shoved Andy off and away from her, standing quickly and picking up her glass of wine, which was gone by the time she felt capable of answering. A second glass was poured by the time she thought she could speak.

There were a thousand things she wanted to say to Andy—the girl who knew everything about her; she had known every kiss, every lover, every secret (apart from one that Rachel had kept hidden deep within her: if it wasn't thought of, wasn't touched, it couldn't matter)—yet no words emerged from her lips.

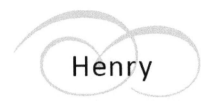

Henry

WHEN HE CLIMBED into the car, the engine was already running, his mother's belt already across her chest. His had barely clicked into place before the car moved and Rachel King's flat disappeared in the rear-view mirror.

He turned to look at his mum as she drove. He even opened his mouth a couple of times. Words poised on the tip of his tongue, contained only by his fear and guilt.

They joined the M20, the journey stretched out before them, but still he couldn't say anything. His mother seemed no more able to break the silence.

Elizabeth

THE NEXT TIME they spoke was when they'd walked through their front door and Henry had kicked off his shoes, not bothering to untie his laces. She was too tired to care about the state of the backs of his shoes, too tired to care that he'd dropped his school bag on a pair of her more expensive heels, too tired to care that he had simply discarded his coat on the floor.

"Go upstairs and get your computer. I'll find room for it on the table in the living room."

"What the fu—?"

"Now."

Henry's mouth opened, a protest sure to be on the tip of his tongue, but the mask she was wearing was enough to silence his thoughts. Instead, he turned on his heel and thundered up the stairs. The sound of his door crashing against its frame reverberated around the house.

A small, timid cough brought her back to where she was standing.

Between leaving work, going to Tesco—shit, the ice cream—and driving to Dover, she'd never remembered to text Sam.

"I had a whole indignant speech about keeping in contact, answering your phone and telling me where you are." Sam looked at her, pity swallowing the colour of his eyes. "But it looks like you've had quite the evening."

She merely took off her coat and scarf and hung them on hooks, picked up Henry's, dusted it off, and hung it beside hers.

"What happened? Where have you been?" His arm was around her and he was leading her further into the house which she had bought with Alex two decades ago, a house she seemed to now share with Sam.

She shook her head.

There was clattering above her, followed swiftly by the sound of Henry swearing loudly and obnoxiously. She wondered when he had started swearing. He'd hadn't sworn in the house since Petr Cech had signed for Arsenal and even that had been PG.

She dropped down on the sofa and kicked off her heels; Sam sat beside her and took her hand in his, but she immediately cast it off.

"What happened tonight?" Sam asked her once more.

Henry entered with the body of his computer, saving her from having to answer; he had always been such an obedient boy.

He looked down to the machine in his hands. She nodded over to the table by the window.

"You know I have a human right to privacy," he told her as he walked his computer to its new home.

"No." She shook her head and took a sip of the beer Sam had open on the coffee table. "You're a British Citizen. Privacy is a privilege. A privilege you have lost."

She put the beer back down on a coaster, something Sam had failed to do.

"I'll go get the rest of the stuff," he said simply, leaving her to Sam.

"Will you please tell me what happened?"

"Just—" She ran her hands through her hair as she contemplated the rest of her sentence. A headache had formed, and it was going to be all consuming. She needed to talk to Henry. The shopping needed unpacking from the boot of her car. That fucking ice cream needed dealing with.

"Why don't you stay at yours tonight?" Sam didn't move. He

looked at her blankly, no, that wasn't it. His face was showing too many emotions to name. Confusion? Hurt? Anger?

"Why are you looking at me like that?"

"Because I'm trying to work out if you're joking," he said, taking back his beer from the table.

"Because you've been drinking?"

"Because I've got tenants."

She was an articulate woman—she could argue to her position in a boardroom full of suits, hold her own in a drunken debate with Matt, even manage to win a couple of fights with her mother, yet no words were coming to mind now.

"Told you he lived here." Henry smirked at her as he wandered in with his monitor, a keyboard tucked under his arm and what appeared to be a mouse hanging out of his pocket.

"Enough. The pair of you," were the words that eventually emerged as she forced her way out of the room and up the stairs.

* * *

For almost all of Henry's life it had just been the two of them. There were suddenly four of them though. Two of them weren't talking to her and the fourth was in a flat in Dover.

She rolled over and found an empty space where a man usually lay beside her. He could be heard snoring from the guest room.

Is Sam going to move in? the question came when she'd asked Henry for his key to loan to Sam.

No, she'd replied quickly, I think our family is quite big enough.

Then why does he need a key?

Because I would quite like my plants to still be alive when we return from your grandmother's.

She threw off the covers and marched across to the wardrobe. Where there had only been her clothes for fifteen years, and a solitary sweater of Alex's, there were now Sam's. Hoodies, shirts, even a suit she'd never seen him in. Alex's solitary sweater nowhere to be seen. Shoving Sam's clothes aside, she found Alex's old cable knit jumper pinned to the edge of the wardrobe, barely holding on to its hanger. She pulled it off the remainder of the way and held it close to her face. She'd hated it on him. It was a foul shade of green, and where the sleeves were coming away from its cuffs, Alex would poke his thumbs through. It hung on him much too loosely. When he was at his worst, he wouldn't take it off. She didn't know why it was this sweater of his she'd chosen to keep.

She pulled it closer still, wrapping it around her shoulders like a shield, wearing it like a talisman, or a physical metaphor for her day. It no longer smelt of him. It smelt of Sam's clothes that had been rubbing against it. Of the detergent she'd bought because it was on offer—she didn't like the fragrance and couldn't wait to finish the box. She tried to remember what Alex smelt like. She'd bought him a bottle of Jean Paul Gaultier one anniversary, she'd fallen in love with the bottle rather than the smell, but he'd never worn it. His preference had always been for Old Spice as his father had worn.

She walked across to the dresser. Sam had a couple of things stored in a drawer for about a year now, a couple of pairs of socks and pants, yet they'd mutated. She pulled open the drawer below and found t-shirts, below that contained trousers and jeans. On top rested a bottle of Dolce and Gabbana missing its top next to a bottle promising to smell like the movie Scarface.

When did this happen?

How had she not noticed?

Her phone glowed on her bedside table and illuminated the room.

03:47: Would it be ok if I saw Henry again? Rachel

Elizabeth didn't like that she hadn't put her surname. That she had assumed she was the only Rachel she would know. She did, however, take comfort in the fact that the other woman, her son's other mother, wasn't sleeping either.

The message lit up the locked screen of her phone. The small light so strong in the night, making shadows that seemed to dance around her room. Her phone faded back to black and she was alone in the darkness once more.

She swapped Alex's jumper for her dressing gown and wrapped it tightly around her; this smelt of Killer Queen. Henry had bought it for Mother's Day last year, knowing that she would not only hate it but that she wouldn't know who Katy Perry was. Henry's smile had been so bright as she'd tried to look pleased with her gift. You have to love it, he'd continued to beam at her, because I got it for you. She'd worn it once, yet the smell lingered.

She pulled her phone free of its charger and padded out of the room.

When she went to check on Henry, she could see lights flickering under the bottom of his door. She thought about going in, but she was worried about the boy she would find. She wanted it to be her son, the boy who'd fall asleep with his hand over her heart, but she feared it would be her teenager, the boy who had two mothers.

She left his door, her palm lightly pressing against its wood, her only contact, and went downstairs. She found a glass of wine and went into her study.

Opening the bottom drawer of the desk, she pulled out all of the family's paperwork. Her marriage certificate, the death certificate, Henry's adoption papers. She looked at the picture of Rachel King and took a long drink from her glass.

How had she not recognised her at the train station? This girl—woman now—had given her the most precious thing in her life. She had given Alex and her a child when she didn't think she'd ever have one. For too short a period of time her family had been complete. She'd had it all.

Elizabeth had drained the glass before she found the courage to unlock her phone. She'd contemplated pouring another before she told her phone to call the unknown number. Barely one ring—it sounded so loudly against her ear she thought it would wake the house—before she hung up. She was a coward, she had always been a coward.

Her phone went flying through the air and it landed awkwardly across the room. She'd hoped it was broken, that she'd have to get a new phone, a new number perhaps. But Henry had bought her an expensive case, and painstakingly applied a screen protector to it. It wouldn't be broken, at best it would be scratched. She was a coward and she had been looking for a coward's way out.

Had she thrown her phone slightly harder, had it turned once more in the air, it would have landed the other way up and Elizabeth wouldn't have seen her phone lighting up once more, she wouldn't have seen Rachel calling her back.

She left her seat at her desk and knelt beside her mobile on the floor. She watched her phone glowing, the eleven numbers on the screen demanding her attention, the other woman awake in the night in her flat in Dover. She wanted so much to be the coward she knew she was. But she also wanted her son to talk to her again. To love her again.

"Hello?"

"I'm sorry if my text woke you."

"I wasn't asleep."

"I looked through the folder Henry made. He's a smart kid."

"He's brilliant."

"I'm sorry about this evening."

"I—" Elizabeth had been conducting the conversation on autopilot. Once again talking to the woman as if she were a parent at one of Henry's football games, or perhaps a colleague in the lift or a hairdresser. The apology rattled her, though. She didn't understand why the woman was asking for forgiveness.

"I should have been harder to find."

Still Elizabeth had nothing to say.

"He's not my child. I'm not his mother. I didn't raise him. I didn't love him. I can't imagine what you're going through."

Elizabeth released the tears she'd been containing. Her phone lay forgotten beside her as she silently sobbed in the early morning.

That was how Sam found her. Lying in a heap on the floor, her knees tucked tightly to her chest, huddled beneath her dressing gown, her phone lying forgotten beside her. Sam had whispered soothing nothings into her ear, complained about how cold she'd let herself become, but he couldn't reach her, he couldn't find her behind the unhappiness.

Sam's arms around her were replaced by Henry's and she finally allowed herself to be comforted. Comforted by her son, her boy, the most loved little man in all the world, she cried anew.

"I'm sorry Mum," he whispered into her hair. "I'm so sorry."

"I know." She nodded, wiping her eyes as she sat up. "I knew this day would come. I just thought—"

"We'd do it together," he finished for her.

She looked down at her phone and pressed the home screen. There were a dozen or so messages waiting to be read, all from Rachel's unknown number. She ignored them and looked at the time. She looked back to her son, his arms still tentatively trying to hold her. Still in his superhero pyjamas. He looked so small, so like the boy that used to fall asleep with his hand over her heart.

"Did you sleep at all last night?"

Henry shook his head.

"What do you want for breakfast?"

"I should get ready for school."

"You'll be late," she told him simply.

"You should get ready for work." His arms were tighter around her.

"I'll be late." She smiled at him.

"Eggie bread."

* * *

They were sitting at the breakfast bar, two empty plates before them, dishes waiting for her in the sink, as the news played softly in the background. Sarah Montague explained the world around them. Syria. Putin. The fallout from those votes that happened so long ago but simply wouldn't go away. Henry concentrated on something untouchable in the distance as he finished the last of his tea.

She remembered a word from a book she'd read. She couldn't remember its title, or even the person who'd written it, all she could remember was a word on one of the pages: *sobremesa*. The author hadn't explained it, just left the word on the paper. She'd had to look it up. It was Spanish and meant the time between finishing a meal and the washing up, just enjoying the company of those you'd shared it with.

Suddenly it all stopped, their small sobremesa rudely interrupted by the front door slamming shut, a reminder that they shared their house with another who was telling them that he had just left without saying a word to either of them.

Elizabeth gathered their plates, put the kettle back on to boil and started running water to do the washing up. Henry busied himself by putting last night's dishes away from whatever Sam had made for his supper. She hadn't yet told Sam how much she disliked dishes being left to dry on the side, how hard it was to get the drip marks off that drainer. Years ago, she'd thought about replacing it, changing it for a material that was easier to clean, but she'd never gotten around to it. She simply put the dishes away as soon as she'd finished washing them. Henry, as he'd grown, had slipped into the habit of drying them up as she went.

He had always been such an obedient child.

They were both still in their pyjamas, and she was making a second cup of coffee, when he finally asked the question she'd been hoping he'd put off for just a little bit longer.

"Are you going to speak to Rachel?"

"We spoke last night." She put the lid back on the milk and placed it in the fridge. "This morning," she corrected.

"What did you talk about?"

"Not much." She wondered how long Rachel King had stayed on the phone listening to her cry. She should look at the messages on her phone. "I'll try again though."

"We could invite her over for supper."

She watched him, his eager anticipation barely contained on his face. "She can't cook. Andy has to cook for her."

"I doubt she had anyone to teach her."

"Like Grandpa taught you? Like you taught me?"

She pulled him in close to her, his coconut shampoo filling her nostrils, unconsciously reminding her of the macaroons she'd tried to teach him to bake. He'd been distracted by a neighbour's cat hunting a bird in the garden, she'd been too busy watching Henry watch the cat, and the macaroons had been left to burn in the oven. Neither of them really liked coconuts anyway. Coconut had always been Alex's favourite.

Rachel

PETE WAS HEADBUTTING her, his front paws pushing his weight uncomfortably down on her chest. She hugged him tightly until he decided he needed to leave, to escape the confines of her arms, letting him think that it was his decision to stop pushing down heavily on her breasts.

She looked around her; there was a note Blu-Tacked to the mirror opposite. She crawled to the edge of her bed, taking her duvet as she went so she could read Andy's tidy yet painfully small writing.

> *I see you made it back into your own bed, you know you could have stayed.*
> *Called in sick to work for you. Told them there was liquid escaping you from every orifice. Should get you a couple of days. Use them wisely, you know Netflix, Xbox, winning the World Cup with Tottenham on Football Manager, that kind of thing.*
> *Thinking of making fajitas for dinner?*
> *Love you, A xx*

She threw herself backwards on the bed and grabbed for her phone, glancing at the time. It was lunchtime, so Andy would be in the staffroom looking up ways to inject caffeine intravenously.

Spurs can't win the world cup. Not a country. Thank you for the vomit though xx

Andy's message back to her came just seconds later: The fact that a) you didn't think I knew that and b) you thought that important enough to text me hurts greatly xx

The text was followed by a picture of an actress coughing into a phone with subtitles reading 'I'm sick.' Rachel knew the still instantly to be from Mean Girls. She was thinking about searching through Netflix for it and watching it in the bath, when a second message came through.

Are you available to talk? Elizabeth.

She hit the information button in the corner and called the number back. One ring and they were talking again.

"I'm sorry about last night."

"I understand." Rachel found herself nodding redundantly. "I spent at least twenty minutes locked in a bathroom yesterday."

"Look . . ." She could picture the steely determination etched across the older woman's face. She found herself swallowing. ". . . if you're to do this, if we're to do this, I need guarantees." The woman sighed down the line. Rachel saw Elizabeth's hands at her temple, rubbing away a headache, trying to rub away her—this new intrusion—from her life. "If you're to do this, you're to do this."

"I don't think I follow." Rachel frowned back at her, instinctively reaching out for Pete back on the bed besides her for comfort.

"You can't come into Henry's life, decide it's too much and leave. Henry . . . as old and as adult as he likes to think he is, he's still just a boy. He's not strong enough to cope with that."

"I—I made a promise to Henry."

"I heard." Elizabeth's tone was firm, business like—every word crisp and calculated as if she had to pay for each one and didn't have money to waste—she was back to the woman who had stood in her doorway, the woman who had called her Ms. King.

The woman who had cried down the phone in the early hours brushed aside and hidden within her.

"You promised you'd talk to me. You have. Your end is fulfilled. If you don't think you can do this, I will make up an excuse for you. But I need to know now, before it's too late, before . . ."

"Before Henry gets hurt," she found herself finishing.

"Indeed."

The silence could be picked apart and chewed upon. Pete nestling himself in her crossed legs gave her a false confidence.

"I know you think I'm some stupid teenager that got knocked up—"

"No, I think you're the woman who entrusted me to raise her child as my own. And that is what I am doing."

"I can do this," Rachel told her firmly. "I just don't know what I can offer him."

"Answers," was the short, sharp reply.

She looked across at the folder he'd given her, thought about all the years she'd spent imagining her own parents: what the three of them might look like in family photographs, how they'd smile at her, all the reasons they might have had for not wanting to be in her life. When she was really small, she would go to bed and fall asleep thinking about how they would come find her.

It was the same every night, they would drive up, knock on the door and introduce themselves. They'd apologise for leaving but THEY'D make it up to her, they'd pack her things into their car and they'd drive away together. She never pictured a house or a life with them, only ever their coming to get her, offering their apologies, their reasons.

"Yeah, I guess so."

"Are you free for dinner tomorrow night?"

"Yeah."

"Okay. Seven o'clock. Do you have any dietary requirements?"

Rachel suddenly felt as though she were booking a seat on a plane. Lacto-vegetarian, Vegan/vegetarian, Asian/Hindu vegetarian, Muslim, Kosher, Diabetic, Gluten intolerant, Low calorie, Low fat, Low salt, Low lactose. All our meals are nut free. Made in a nut free factory. Cannot guarantee nut free.

"No. I'm fairly easy going when it comes to food."

"Good. Given my misadventure with pens." She felt Elizabeth relaxing into the conversation just as it was ending. "I'll text you our address."

"I don't have a car."

"If you can get to Wye train station, I'll pick you up. Just let me know what time you're due to arrive."

"Thank you."

"I will see you tomorrow, Ms. King."

"Rachel, my name is Rachel."

"I will see you tomorrow, Rachel." Her name was repeated back to her, it was delivered slowly and deliberately, as if it had been a battle that Elizabeth had to fight to be able to produce the two syllables of her name. Rach. El.

With that the phone call was ended and all she could hear was Pete purring softly in her lap. She swapped her phone for the remote on her bedside table, wrapped the duvet back around her, trying not to disturb the cat, and flicked on the television.

* * *

She was woken by Andy climbing into bed beside her, the wool of her jumper scratching across her own bare arms.

"How was work?" Rachel mumbled into her pillow.

"Terrible, my TA is off with the norovirus. Tyler kept wiping his snotty nose on my arm and Stephanie wet herself again. Luckily it was during P.E., so I could just throw her back in her uniform and push her towards her mother."

"Is Helen vomiting from every orifice too?"

"Where do you think I got the idea?"

Rachel rolled over to face her. Andy still had her glasses on and hadn't bothered to take off her lanyard, *Miss A. Grigoriadis, Reception Class Teacher*. She fiddled with the plastic of her picture, Andy hated it, thinking she looked old and stuffy, too much like her mother; Rachel thought she looked wonderful in it, one of the few photographs in her dark rims.

"Aside from that though?" Rachel let the picture drop between them.

"Good day. I think we've got the number six down." Andy's breath blew a warm breeze across her face, smelling of coffee as always.

"It's only October and you're going to have to invest in a bigger die." She looked up and met Andy's eyes. Brown, in tandem with the darkness of her hair.

"I know everything about you, and you me. We've traded stories like friendship bracelets. I told you about losing my virginity to Kyle, so you told me about Charlotte. You told me about that time in hospital, so I told you about my dad's temper." The sheet was pulled up high, it was as though they were exchanging secrets at a sleepover. "How come you never told me you had a child?"

Rachel thought of all the ways she could respond to that comment, pushing most of them away before settling on: "I probably never would have, it wasn't exactly my finest hour."

Andy closed the gap between them and laid a tender kiss across her lips.

"Why are you kissing me now?" Rachel asked as her hand played with the hem of Andy's jumper. She wanted so badly to free her of it, to feel the other woman close to her, to just forget everything that had happened.

"Because you need it."

She rolled away from her friend and out of bed. She found her jogging bottoms and quickly covered herself, suddenly all too aware that she was naked all but the old t-shirt she'd been sleeping in.

"Where are you going?"

"You're back from work, so it's coffee time."

Rachel turned to find Andy sitting up, hugging her knees close to her chest, hair ruffled from the pillow, glasses slightly askew. She was never turned down, Rachel always accepted her advances as a gift, never knowing when she would receive them again.

"I know what I said wrong last night, but what did I say this time?" Andy spoke softly and to her knees.

Rachel shook her head. She didn't want to have this conversation, she never did, but they'd been putting if off for so long now it was forever in the room with them; the words left unsaid took up so much space their small two-bedroom flat.

"Just once," she found herself sitting on the bed again, back to Andy, eyes longing to find something out of the window that would warrant an instant end to the conversation, "when I ask you that question, I'd like to you reply that you're kissing me simply because you want to. Because you can."

There was nothing out of the window though, nothing that could pull her attention away from the woman in her bed, wrapped so tightly amongst her limbs. So small, so fragile.

"What if I don't? What if I never do?" Andy's voice was tender and her words tentative.

Rachel turned slowly, her t-shirt caught under her legs, revealing more of her than she wanted. She was always naked before Andy anyway.

"I love you."

"And I love you too." Andy's forehead was a labyrinth of lines, unable to understand the statement put before her.

"But how do you love me? Do you love me like you loved Jesse or like you love Florence? Like one of your million sisters? Like *Pete*?"

Andy didn't say anything, but relaxed her legs and lay Rachel's head into her lap, her fingers running laps in her hair.

"I don't know how long we can keep doing this," Rachel finally released.

"I know."

Andy continued to comb.

"I haven't been with anyone else since Nick Clegg was considered decent."

"I hated that self-righteous, Liberal Democrat, Alternative Vote pushi—"

"Tasha hated you too."

"Is that why things ended?" Andy moved her face, so Rachel was forced to look up at her. "Because I always thought I did very well at being civil to her."

"She dumped me. She told me that she couldn't be with anyone that looked at another the way I looked, I look," she corrected, "at you."

"And how do you look at me?"

"Like . . ." Rachel closed her eyes and tried to remember the worst parts of their friendship. All the drunken spats, the sober arguments, the nights of crying and days trapped under the duvet for fear of getting out of bed, the stays back in Epping, the fact she had her own toothbrush and drawer full of clothes at Marc's.

All those memories were swallowed up by the stolen moments Andy allowed them: the drugged-up trysts, barely able to call to mind; the encounters after one too many beers, replaced by one too many glasses of wine as Andy's tastes had changed; the weekends of comfort that only Rachel could offer, after whichever latest relationship ended; the week in bed they'd shared when Andy had run from Laszlo's engagement ring.

Why are you kissing me?

Because I'm not a wife.

The longest Rachel had been granted was a month two summers

ago. Andy had broken up for six weeks and, by the second, she was bored. She'd persuaded Rachel to cash in all her annual leave and booked them on a flight—seemingly arbitrarily—to Zagreb. At the airport she'd picked up a copy of *Lonely Planet* and they toured the coast and flown out of Federico Fellini airport (apologising profusely for wasting their last full day in San Marino). Each night Andy had crept into her bed and stayed there until the sunlight woke them. She would roll over in the mornings, forcing their bodies out of the positions they'd slept in—Andy resting on the shelf of Rachel's knees—kiss her awake and tell them what they'd be doing that day.

Rachel had spent that month following Andy around in a daze, not noticing the cathedrals, the museums or galleries, simply waiting until she would find Andy crawling besides her, in the single bed of whatever hostel they'd found for that evening and explore her body a fresh.

Why are you kissing me?

Because we're on holiday.

"I would give you an onion," Rachel eventually admitted, looking up at Andy.

They had been stoned the first time they'd heard those words, giggling in the corner of a pub as Marc sat beside them quoting Carol Ann Duffy at a PGCE student far too good for him. Andy had put on a thick Scottish accent and started repeating lines from *Shrek*, Rachel had pretended to be Eddie Murphy. Marc had taken the boy he was trying to impress to the bar for another drink. Andy had taken her back to the flat she shared with Florence and they'd watched the film on repeat, fresh laughter escaping from them every time onions were mentioned. *Why are you kissing me? Because I'm stoned.*

When Rachel had woken the next morning, she'd found a text from Marc: I *should start paying Ms Duffy royalties*. She'd texted him back asking for the name of the poem. *Valentine,* had been his simple reply before a torrent of messages about the PGCE student's performance, length and girth. She'd nearly text him back with a report of her own, but at that point Andy was still her secret; if she told anyone, Andy might stop, and she wasn't ready for it to stop.

Andy pushed her away. "You're such a lesbian," she scolded before pulling her back, her fingers playing along her collar bone. Rachel felt her pulse weaken with every gentle touch. "What do you want to do?" she asked Rachel softly.

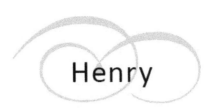

Henry

HENRY FIRST WATCHED *High Fidelity* when he was fourteen. Alyssa had taken him by the hand and led him into her brother's room, *He's away at university. Warwick*, Henry had been told as Alyssa pushed him onto the old single bed. Her parents were still at work. Her brother's TV/VHS combo was the only one left in the house. She'd slipped in the dusty video and they'd sat and watched it on the absent brother's old *Star Wars* duvet set, their backs rigid against the cold wall, hands inching closer together until their little fingers were joined.

He was tense for the entirety of the 114-minute running time. As the video began to rewind, she'd encouraged his hand onto her thigh, kissed him on very edge of his mouth and told him that they should watch other Nick Hornby films. She'd heard good things about *An Education*.

When Henry got home, he'd dug out his Kindle from underneath his bed and downloaded as many of Nick Hornby's books as he thought he could get away with before his mother noticed the money coming out of her account. Determined to become an expert, to impress Alyssa with his extensive knowledge, to trade facts, movie quotes and favourite pages for kisses and touches.

He read *Fever Pitch* first, but rushed through it, believing that a book about football would not be the best way to a girl's heart. He followed that with *High Fidelity*, following the plot a lot more easily on the page without a girl pressed against his side, picturing himself as Rob Gordon and starting to punctuate every conversation with a list.

Top five favourite books.
Top five Arsenal players sold too soon.
Top five reasons given to Mr. Scott for forgetting my homework.
Top five songs that remind me of Alyssa.

It was a habit that was as short lived as Alyssa's interest in Nick Hornby, except for when it came to films.

Top five superhero films.
Top five films from the 90s.
Top five films made before I was born.
Top five Lucasfilm films.

After his mum had explained to him what a personal day was, Henry decided that they should sit and watch one of his lists. He'd initially planned on *Top five Matthew Broderick films,* so they could watch *Ferris Bueller's Day Off*. He opted against that choice when he realised that, to be true to his list, they would have to watch *Election*, and he didn't feel comfortable watching that with his mother.

He settled on *Top five films starring robots*. They'd watched *Terminator 2: Judgement Day* and *Big Hero 6,* about to start on *The Hitchhikers Guide to the Galaxy* when she stepped out of the room. He thought her grip on her mobile might be enough to bend it. It had annoyed him that she'd been texting through most of *Big Hero 6*, even more that she'd not been watching for the Baymax fist bump bit.

He looked at his watch, it was lunchtime, so she would have left to call Sam on his break to continue their fevered conversation through voice rather than thumbs.

He slipped out from under the blanket she'd pulled out of the boiler cupboard for them. *All movie days have to happen under blankets.* He'd thought about all the *Star Wars* marathons he'd made her endure, all the *Disney* films, all the one-star reviewed films on Netflix he'd forced her to watch because they were so bad, they were bound to be good. All of them were under the fraying navy blanket that he couldn't remember them ever not having.

He slipped into the hallway and stood by the open door of her study. Even without her mobile on speakerphone, he could hear both sides of the conversation. She always had her phone volume excessively loud. She'd told him that she'd damaged her hearing when she was in her early twenties listening to her Walkman. She constantly nagged him whenever he had earphones in as a consequence.

"Are you coming back?"

Henry didn't need to peer round the doorframe to know she would be sitting at her desk, the hand supporting her head subconsciously playing with her hair.

"Seeing as you didn't realise I'd moved in," was Sam's reply.

Silence. She would be chewing her lip now.

"We had discussed it."

"When?"

"When I told you about what Marcus had been telling me about how his estate agents are always looking for new landlords, about the money they make. How did you think I'd managed to afford Arsenal tickets? Do you have any idea how much it costs to take a family of four to the Emirates for a Premier League game?"

"I thought—"

"What? What did you think, Elizabeth?"

Henry stepped away. This wasn't a conversation for his ears, it hadn't been all the while he'd been listening, but it suddenly felt so much worse.

He went into the kitchen to make them both a fresh drink. While he waited for the kettle, he rummaged in the back of the cupboards, hoping to find some microwavable popcorn that they'd both forgotten about. There was none. Crisps would have to do.

She joined him as he was throwing away his tea bag.

"Rachel will be joining us for supper tomorrow."

The bag fell from the spoon to the floor. He scurried to put it in the right place. She joined him on the floor with a paper towel, clearing away the drops of tea from the wet bag.

"I'm sorry, I should have asked."

"No, that's cool. That's better than cool. I just wasn't expecting you to be so cool about it."

He didn't know why he was using the word 'cool' so much. He didn't think he'd used that word since he was in primary school.

"I'm cool." His mother frowned at him, throwing away the piece of kitchen roll and taking her cup of coffee from the counter.

"Mum, you are many things, but I don't think you've ever been cool."

"I'll have you know for my twenty-first birthday your father got me tickets to see *Top of the Pops* being recorded. We saw Oasis."

"That would make Dad cool, not you."

"Hmmm." She blew into her coffee.

He stood beside her and opened his bag of crisps.

"Is Sam coming back?" he asked after a while. His words punctuated with the taste of Cheese and Onion on his tongue.

"Do you want him to come back?"

He didn't know the answer, so he replaced her question with another of his: "Does he know I'm adopted?"

"There's nothing to say about your adoption," she said after a while. "You're my son. No amount of stretch marks, labour pains and life-threatening agony could change that."

"Does he know about Dad?"

"I think the wedding photo on my dresser would have given him a pretty good indication."

Henry rolled his eyes. His mother was always honest with him, but some days it took her longer to get to the truth than others. She never lied, she was just evasive. A trait he hoped he wouldn't inherit but sensed would come to him anyway.

"No."

He swallowed his mouth full of crisps; he wanted to say the next bit carefully. He wanted to make sure there would be no excuse for her not to hear him.

"That Dad had depression. About his accident."

"He knows your father died. He knows you were just a baby at the time. We haven't discussed it any more than that. There's nothing more to say."

"Was it an accident?" he asked, hoping his voice sounded braver then he was feeling.

He watched as she carefully put her coffee back down on the counter. As she wrapped her fingers around the edge of the counter, her knuckles slowly turned white. She was still in her pyjamas; he didn't remember the last time she'd spent all day in her pyjamas, even when she'd picked up the flu from her office, she'd got dressed every day she had off work.

"Your father loved us very much," was all she gave him by way of an answer.

"He doted on us," he said eventually, finishing the line from his stories they'd said together as a child.

He dropped his crisp packet on the counter and leant his head on her shoulder. He was taller than her now. He wrapped his hand, greasy and dusty from his crisps, around hers. That too was bigger.

"Grab your coffee, we've got Marvin the Paranoid Android to watch before we can get onto *RoboCop*."

"Which version?"

He didn't dignify that with a response, just pulled at her hand and grabbed for his tea before leading her back into the living room as if he were still a boy.

* * *

She was asleep by the time he got onto *Star Wars*. He had updated the list and replaced *Episode IV* for *VII*. He often debated whether he should include *Star Wars* in his *Top five films with robots* as *Star Wars* was a list of its own and meant excluding other great films with robots. *Blade Runner* had to be moved to *Top five dystopian films*. However, it was *Star Wars* and there was no way he could have a *Top five films with robots* without at least one of them.

As he turned away from Han Solo's death at the hands of his son, as he did every time, he caught his mother sleeping beside him, her legs curled under her, head resting on her arm uncomfortably on the side of the sofa. He wanted her to be awake for this bit. He wanted her to see how, as much as they both denied it, blood played a part in everyone's lives. It forged their identities.

She had seen the scene before though. He had made her watch it countless times. Twice in the cinema alone. She had told him that he'd wear out the tape. He didn't understand the reference. He knew about videos and cassettes, but he didn't understand how the film or music could fade away. He certainly didn't understand what a pencil had to do with them.

He wondered if Rachel had grown up with videos and cassettes. If she knew what the pencil was for. She was nine years younger than his mother. Did that mean she was in the pencil generation too?

He turned from his mother to the screen. Rey and Kylo Ren were fighting in the woods now. Light side verses dark. Kylo fighting his uncle's, his grandfather's, light sabre. Blood was the link. Blood was always the link.

Henry didn't want blood to be important though. He didn't want that to be his identity. He wanted it to be nurture over nature. But blood had to be important, had to play a part, otherwise she and his dad wouldn't have adopted him in the first place. If they weren't scared of his father's blood, they would have had a child of their own.

But he *was* their child.

He was brilliant. Like his father had been brilliant.

Henry wanted her to be awake, he wanted her to be watching this with him. He wanted her to know why he went searching for Rachel. Why he was putting her through this hurt. He wanted to know about her. Had to know about her. To see if she was sad, like his father had been sad.

Elizabeth

HENRY CAME DOWNSTAIRS with his uniform on, his tie waiting to be knotted around his neck. She was still in her pyjamas and dressing gown, her only acknowledgement to starting the new day was the cup of coffee in her hand.

"I thought you might want to stay home from school today, perhaps you have a *Top five films with Brad Pitt*?"

"Gross," Henry told her while grabbing an apple from the bowl, "besides, you don't like *Fight Club*, so there would be little point."

"I just want to keep you close," she admitted, putting her cup down so she could wrap her arms around him. She wasn't wearing any heels, she didn't like that he was taller than her now.

"Everyone will complain that I'm bunking if I take the last day of term off."

"Let them complain."

"I'll need to get the notes from my classes yesterday."

"You're smart enough to catch up without them."

He rearranged their bodies so he was hugging her now and bent his head, so he could whisper in her ear. "I'm going to school, Mum, I promise," a kiss to her forehead, "I'm not going to Dover."

She stopped protesting and made him a cup of tea to drink as she prepared him a packed lunch, something she'd not done for him in years, sending him to school with a kiss on the cheek.

"School, Mum, not Rachel's. Stop being weird." He wiped the kiss away.

She watched him walk down the road and to the bus stop from the front step before heading into her study and waking her computer.

She'd checked her messages (there weren't any) and her work emails before setting another Out of Office.

Thank you for your email.

Sorry I'm not in the office today, I'm sat at home wondering what to cook for my son's birth mother and if my boyfriend is coming back.

If it's urgent, I'm still not going to deal with it before Monday.

She didn't like the word boyfriend, Sam wasn't her boyfriend. She was forty-two, he was forty-seven, Sam's ex-wife was thirty-one and Rachel was thirty-three. She was too old to have a boyfriend.

Alex would be forty-three now, forty-four in March, this February would mark the sixteenth anniversary of his death. She was too young to be a widow.

Elizabeth changed her Out of Office to something sensible, told whoever emailed her that she would be back in on Monday, then sent a text to Sam telling him she was going out. If he wanted to get any of his things for the weekend, she reminded him that Isaac's favourite plastic dinosaur remained on the dining room table. A stegosaurus sat neatly at one end, waiting to be fed. Then she headed for the shower.

In the car she called to let Caitlin know she was coming over. She listened to BBC Radio 4 as she drove, a documentary about the laws tightening abortion across Europe. Thoughts turning to a seventeen-year-old girl sixteen years ago and the small life she was carrying. *She's a lesbian, Mum, is that why she didn't want me?* Thoughts turning to her son's conception. *Do you think that's why she's a lesbian? Because she got pregnant?*

Sexuality doesn't work like that, was her meagre reply. She changed the channel to BBC Radio 2 and hoped their topic of conversation would be a safer one.

When she pulled into Caitlin's driveway, she thought about turning around and going home, but her wheels had affected the gravel and the front door was already opening, and Thatcher was already bounding towards her car.

She turned off the engine and slowly opened the door, the dog quickly inside, demanding his head be rubbed as he soppily threw it into her lap. She turned and grabbed her handbag, glad to see Caitlin holding him by his collar so she could step out in peace.

"Why aren't you at work?" Caitlin asked her as she kissed each cheek, Thatcher still struggling to be included in the welcome.

"Wanted to see my friend, see how she's doing," Elizabeth replied as she followed her into the house. "Count the trees in Sevenoaks, play with some cats in aforementioned friend's cattery."

"Our friendship is older than my teeth, don't bullshit me. There are eight oaks, as well you know." Caitlin took her coat and hung it above the umbrellas in the hall before leading her into the kitchen. "And you have never played. Why aren't you at work?" Caitlin asked again, flicking switches on her coffee machine.

"Personal day," Elizabeth sat down at the island and started thumbing through the newspaper splayed out across the kitchen table.

"You haven't taken a personal day since . . ."

"You can say his name; it's been fifteen years."

Elizabeth continued to turn the pages, her eyes hovering too long over more news of abortion laws changing. Had Rachel ever considered an abortion?

"What's going on with you? I see you've redecorated. Matt will complain."

"Matt lives to complain, hence constantly away lobbying the European Commission."

A latte was placed in front of her. "More importantly, why are you here?" Caitlin asked, tidying away *The Guardian* as she sat beside her, her cappuccino ready to be forgotten and left to go cold.

"Henry tracked down his birth mother. I'm cooking supper for her later." Elizabeth hoped her voice conveyed the tone of nonchalance she was aiming for, as if she were simply ticking items off a shopping list. "Sam isn't talking to me and he may have moved out because I wasn't aware that he'd moved in. Did you know he'd moved in?"

She watched Caitlin fiddle with the cup; Caitlin didn't really drink coffee any more, she simply liked having a cup before her. She just needed something to fiddle with: a hangover from quitting smoking when she and Matt had tried for a baby; the miscarriages enough to strengthen her vow to never take it up again.

"Where to start." Caitlin smiled sadly at her.

Both women looked out to the garden, where Thatcher was chasing a bird, bouncing about on the lawn as if he were still a puppy.

"We saw her at St Pancras when Sam had taken us to watch Arsenal play."

"Henry still not talking around him?"

"He's mostly fine when it's an Isaac weekend, it's when it's just the three of us he freezes up and shuts down. He doesn't like him."

"I don't think you do particularly—"

Her hand was upon Caitlin's, stopping her from spinning the cup any more. As much as Elizabeth loved her, the conversation was a trying one, the constant rattling of the cup on its saucer wasn't helping, especially if Caitlin was planning on remaining this candid.

"They were waiting for me outside the toilets. She—"

"The birth mother?"

Elizabeth nodded. "She was waiting there too. As she walked passed, Henry grabbed her arm."

"His curiosity is going to get him killed one day."

"Or win him a Nobel Prize."

"How is it that you come to be cooking for the woman?"

"This," Elizabeth found herself smiling in spite of the conversation, "is the best bit. Wednesday night I get a phone call, transpires that while I thought Henry was at football, he had actually gone to her flat in Dover."

She paused to allow Caitlin to pull a distasteful face at the thought of her godson in the port town.

"He was eating pasta with her and her flatmate when I got there. He asked if he could see her again and I ended up inviting her over for supper. You know how I get when I'm stressed, I turn into the perfect middle-class woman my mother always wanted."

Elizabeth watched as Caitlin opened and closed her mouth, clearly consciously considering what she was going to say; however, Caitlin said nothing, the hand she laid on Elizabeth's arm all she could offer to assuage. They sat there quietly, eyes back on the dog playing in the garden. Eventually, Caitlin gave her back the paper to go through; they did the crossword together as if they were back at university and looking for things to put off writing essays.

"I think it's over with Sam," she told her once Caitlin had returned from letting in the dog.

"I think you were only with him for Isaac. You love that boy more than you love the father." Caitlin opened a cupboard and revealed to Thatcher his treats, causing his tail to hit anything and everything it came into contact with. "You've always wanted more children."

Caitlin went back to the coffee machine. She fussed the dog. Only when a fresh drink was put in front of her did Caitlin speak again.

"I can't believe you didn't know he'd moved in. You had us round to celebrate."

"We had you round for Matt's fortieth."

"There was Champaign."

"There's always Champaign where Matt's involved."

"Matt doesn't think you like him," Caitlin said after a while.

"Henry said something similar."

"I explained that you don't like anyone."

"I like plenty of people." Elizabeth scowled back. "I like you, Henry—"

"You don't like Matt."

"I like you," she finished needlessly, turning her attention to Thatcher and the patch of drool he was leaving on her leg.

* * *

Driving home she called Sam. He answered the phone unnecessarily quickly, as if he had been waiting for her. She focussed on the road ahead of her and she let Sam fill the silence of the car.

"Do you want me to come back tonight?"

She definitely hadn't expected that. She was hoping for a *hello* or a *how are you?* to warm up with.

"I'll take your silence as a 'no'." He sounded so disappointed in her, as if he'd truly believed that one night at his brother's would have fixed everything. That she'd be begging for his return.

She didn't know if he was being naive or her in calling him so soon.

"Marcus said I can keep the spare room. I'll swap weekends with Mariel and hopefully we'll take Isaac next weekend. The boys can play football in the garden."

She didn't like that Sam was clearly using his son to try and get back into her house. She definitely didn't like that Sam was going from ultimatums one day to painfully accommodating the next. She wondered if this was why his wife had left him, the fact that he could be so many different people. Or was it the fact that Muriel was sixteen years his junior? A whole Henry.

She briefly considered just telling Sam everything: the adoption sixteen years ago and Henry's stalking of the birth mother now. But keeping this secret, hiding away Henry and Alex, seemed so much more important than honesty in this moment. Explaining to Sam about Henry, about Rachel, felt like a betrayal of Alex. It *would* be a betrayal to Alex.

Henry was Alex's child, Alex's son.

Alex would have loved the man their boy was becoming and been so proud of all his achievements. He would have already picked out universities with him, taken him for weekends in Oxford and Cambridge, been punting as they discussed the pros and cons of various colleges and their famous alumni, who they found funnier, Fry or Laurie. They would have spent summers in Edinburgh at The Fringe. They would have spent months in Scotland preparing for the vote.

Alex had wanted to name him David. *He will be king,* he'd told her as they lay in bed one night. He had watched her try to rack her brain for a King David but couldn't find one in her basic knowledge of British history. He had kissed her softly and told her the story of David the King of Israel. *He was a poet and musician, skilled in battle and law. Said to have been of God's own heart.* She just shook her head and rolled over, her back pressed against his chest, his arm pulled tight across her. *He will be Henry Alexander Cole.* He'd pulled her closer still and nodded his agreement into her hair. *Our boy will be king regardless.*

The conversation happened countless times, mostly as they lay awake in bed, sometimes there would be Shakespeare, *a rose by any other name,* other times they would make love thinking of the family they would build and the love they would share. It always ended the same way though, her ear pressed to his chest, listening to the steady rhythm of his heartbeat, a slow finger toying with the hairs between his belly button and crotch, a finger of his own tracing circles behind her ear.

Henry was Alex's child. Explaining to Sam about Henry's adoption, about the sudden arrival of Rachel King—nominative determination Alex had called it, *our boy will be king regardless.* A man that believed in facts and science, tangible evidence, beamed when he saw her name on the paper suddenly preaching about providence: *We would always have been gifted with her child—* would chip away at that. Sam would ask questions she couldn't answer, wouldn't answer for fear of losing the last piece of Alex that she had. That Sam would separate Henry from Alex by taking away the blood they didn't share.

Caitlin's hushed goodbye in her ear, rang loud in her ears. *Either let Sam into your life completely or let him go.*

It had been easy with Sam, he came and went; he was kind and gentle.

Alex had never been easy, everything with him had been a battle. Yes, he had doted on her, would have given her the world if only she'd asked for it, but it was seldom easy. They would watch the news and argue, they would sit in silence for hours, neither one wanting to back down from their stance. There were topics that were off limits because there was no way they could have a civil discussion about them, no way they could talk without wanting to throw something at each other. They could have a fight that would last for hours about whose responsibility it was to buy milk. Then, there were times she would lose him—seemingly for weeks—to his studies, to his thoughts, to the world within his head. But they always needed to be around each other, to feel the other in their proximity. Without the other in bed beside them they wouldn't be able to sleep. As if separated they might forget how to breathe. Their bodies sought each other out, there had to be contact, often as little as their smallest toes touching was enough to know that the other was there.

It was always easy with Sam, but she found that she didn't care enough about Sam to try now that it was getting complicated.

* * *

She'd gone to the supermarket and picked up the ingredients for supper; though she was sure she had most of them at home already, she wanted to be prepared. There were enough unknowns about the meal ahead of them without fretting about the cooking. It was only halfway round Tesco that she remembered that Henry had had pasta just two nights before. Lasagna—his favourite—wouldn't be good for him despite the fact he'd eat pasta every night of the week if she let him. She looked around the aisle, checking she was alone, before putting down her basket and heading back to the start.

New basket. New ingredients. New meal. Shepherd's Pie. Henry's second pick.

Top five favourite meals of Henry Alexander Cole:

> *5. Thai Green Curry (fish, not chicken)*
> *4. Peri-Peri Chicken (Nando's preferably, but yours is just as good, Mum)*
> *3. Roast Dinner (any meat as long as there's Yorkshires and gravy thick enough to hold up a spoon)*
> *2. Shepherd's Pie (potato to the side, not on top)*
> *1. Lasagne (beef sausage rather than mince)*

She wondered how many meals they would have together, how many visits before Rachel learnt all these things, all of Henry's likes and dislikes, his oddities hidden amongst his desire to be like 'every other teenager'. How long it would take for her to catch up on the sixteen lost years, if Henry even wanted her to know everything— when he'd learnt to ride a bike, when he'd stopped believing in Father Christmas, when he'd had his first kiss—or if he would just allow her the merest window into his life. *This is the son you could have had*, a voice that sounded like Cilla Black called out in her head.

Cilla Black wasn't her name though, she had been Priscilla White.

Maybe Henry would change his name too, he would become the King his father had prophesied.

She placed the bag on the counter and glanced at the clock: Henry should be finishing school soon. It was too late to offer him a lift home, she'd never make it through Ashford's traffic in time. Instead, she turned the radio up, changing the pre-set from Radio 4 to 6 Music and let the music fall away as she prepared a meal she wasn't sure anyone would eat.

Rachel

SHE'D BEEN THE only one to get off the train in Wye. She looked around the sleepy station and wondered which side she needed to be on to find Elizabeth. It was dark now, the station bathed in an orange glow of the street lights; British Summer Time would be ending soon, and year to year she could never remember if that meant that it would get slightly lighter for a bit in the evenings before winter finally set in.

Tiny stations like this always reminded her of a scene from *Bedknobs and Broomsticks*, David Tomlinson trying to sleep as the Nazis invaded. Rachel had watched that film curled in Judi's arms, snot and nastiness dripping from her nose. Judi whispering memories of watching it with the twins when they were ill as rhinos raced around a football pitch. *Milner 9.* The child's football shirt hidden beneath her bed surpassed all the other memories.

Her pocket started ringing and she saw the unknown of Elizabeth's number.

The image of the football shirt, *Milner 9,* disappeared and was replaced by the eleven digits of Elizabeth's phone number. She should probably save it. Seventeen years ago, they had communicated through letters and social workers, now they were speaking directly, they were in each other's lives again; she should probably save the woman's number.

"Hi," Rachel looked around for the woman on the other end of the phone, "I have no idea where I'm meant to go."

"Cross the platform, you'll find me in the car park."

She looked across and saw Elizabeth leaning against the side of her car picking something off her scarf, clearly unaware she'd been spotted.

"Hi," the only word emerging from her as Rachel stood face to face with the hard woman that had adopted her baby.

Rachel had no idea why she was here. No idea why she'd agreed to any of this.

Answers.

But she didn't have any.

"It's open." Elizabeth nodded to the other side of her car. "Henry's waiting at home, I left him in charge of the potatoes."

"Cool," Rachel tried again, for lack of anything more substantial to say.

They drove through the village and out the other side, stopping to pull into—what Rachel assumed—must have been the last house before the land was given up to fields and farmers. She'd never lived in a big city, but she'd certainly never lived in an area as rural as this, an area that demanded a car just to buy a pint of milk.

She watched as Elizabeth moved to get out the car, pulling at the handle with her hand before snapping it back to her. Elizabeth turned her head to face Rachel, her features still lit by the mirror light. She was biting her lip—almost childlike.

"I should warn you," she said eventually. "Henry asks a lot of questions."

"Yeah." Rachel nodded. Though he hadn't asked much of her, Andy had told her about the boy's countless questions. Rachel had assumed that tonight it would be her turn, why else had she been called upon. The meal a façade for the true meaning of her visit.

Answers.

But she didn't have any.

"It's a bit heavy going if you're not used to it. I've tried to explain that not everyone will answer his questions."

"I get it, he's inquisitive."

"Caitlin came up with a buzzer system when he was small." Elizabeth's brow knitted slightly as if she was trying to find the best way to explain it. "She just kind of makes a noise, like if you get something wrong on a quiz show, and he knows that he needs to move on. He's asked something inappropriate. My father simply puts his hand up if he doesn't want to answer." She looked back at the house, shaking her head as if none of the conversation mattered. Elizabeth's hand returned to the handle. "Ready?"

Rachel wasn't sure if she was being asked the question or if the other woman was steeling herself for the evening.

The porch light clicked on as they walked along the driveway.

"You've got a beautiful home."

"Thank you, we bought it in '96 back before the market really picked up again."

Rachel smiled at the very Britishness of her sentence, the gut reaction to compliment; play it down and apologetically offer an explanation for it.

"Do you want me to take my shoes off?" she asked, looking at the shoe rack in the porch.

"Most of downstairs has the original stone tiling." Elizabeth shook her head. "You'll freeze."

Following through a second door she found herself in a dining room with an oak table and chairs sitting upon a rug—she knew that Andy would be able to whisper the style into her ear, but without her present the rug was just a rug and the table was just a table—open stairs running up the side of the room which offered a small glimpse of the second floor. She followed Elizabeth through to the kitchen and found Henry, as promised, mashing potatoes.

He looked up and smiled when he saw them.

"Good journey?" he asked, as any well-trained young man would.

"Yes, thank you."

"Can I get you a drink? Wine?" Elizabeth asked her, after putting the meal back on to heat.

"Yes please. Red, if you have some." She watched Elizabeth rummage through a wine rack built into one of the units, the woman inspecting the labels, looking at origin and vintage no doubt. Rachel realised she didn't care. It was Andy that liked wine, it was Andy that had declared, sometime after her twenty-fifth birthday, that they should move on from beer and spirits. "You know what?" Rachel stopped her. "A beer would be better."

Elizabeth stood up tall, a wine bottle in hand. "Are you sure? My friend's partner works in Belgium, always brings me back the most wonderful Pinot noir from Wallonia."

"Yeah." Rachel shook her head, aware she was allowing herself to be told what to do once more. "Sounds great."

"Mum, get her a beer, I think Sam has some left."

"Sam? Is he the, uh, Nottingham Forrest fan?"

"I knew you were listening on the train." Henry smiled, somewhat triumphantly.

"And I was hoping you hadn't seen me." She'd hung her coat up on the back of one of the chairs as Elizabeth handed her a capped bottle of beer. Rachel looked at the label, it was also Belgian.

"So," Henry looked between them both as the silence grew, "this is, like, really awkward, isn't it?"

"Yup." Rachel nodded and took a swig from the bottle.

She watched Elizabeth pour a glass of the red she'd found, her back towards them both, steadying herself against the counter. Her shoulders relaxed as if she put on a new persona, getting ready to act her way through the meal. Elizabeth turned around slowly, her glass now in hand, and smiled at them both, clearly over her stage fright and ready for her performance.

"I was going to say we'd eat out in the dining room, but—"

"It gets really cold." Henry gestured to the mats he'd laid out on a smaller wooden table the other side of the island. "You like shepherd's pie, right?"

"I can never remember the difference between Shepherd's and Cottage."

"Shepherd's is traditionally lamb. Sheep. Shepherds." He was putting spoonfuls of mash onto their three plates. "But Mum makes hers with pork, so I guess it's kind of redundant."

"That, and Henry likes his potato on the side, not on the top," she carried a frying pan over and plated up the rest of the meal, "so it's not really shepherd's pie at all. It's just mince and potato."

Rachel looked at the concoction she was being served and wondered how many families had meals they called one thing but turned out to be, after years of honing and tweaking for preference, something else entirely. She wondered if she could have had this, perhaps with her own mother, maybe with Henry if she'd been older when she'd fallen pregnant. She thought of the meals she'd eaten growing up. Having always adored food, she ate without complaint, without questioning. Perhaps one of those had been an old family favourite without any bearing on its namesake. She thought of Andy, of all the meals she'd cooked for her; maybe one of those meals was something called something else.

"But it's awesome!" Henry took the first two plates over to the table and gestured for Rachel to sit down. "I thought you might bring Andy," he told her quietly as they waited for Elizabeth to join them, "she seemed to talk more than you do."

"I had thought about it—"

"But you're not a couple." It came out more as a question than the statement she thought he intended it to be, as if he weren't sure that was how to describe them.

She nodded, taking a longer sip of her beer. "We're not a couple."

She wondered how much would be socially acceptable to drink before she came across as rude, wondered if there even were any rules for a meal of this design, social etiquette for eating between the son given away and the woman that took him in and promised to love him.

As the three of them sat at the small table, pushing around the meat and potatoes, they teetered on the edge of silence. Every time one of them was about to fall, they were pulled back by a mundane question about work or school. The topic of football—Arsenal versus Spurs, who would win the league this season, Pep Guardiola, Ole Gunnar Solskjær—got them through to the plates being cleared away. Elizabeth led them for a little while about Rachel's job, Brexit, worries that the company would move back to Belgium. But then the cliff's edge began to crumble again and there was nothing left to save them except for the subject they were all avoiding.

When Elizabeth put a cup of coffee down in front of her, Rachel bit the bullet, hoping the trembling of her hand was only noticeable to her. "Andy was saying that you were asking about me, uh . . ." Her hand was at the back of her neck, scratching at the fine hairs that escaped her pony tail. "You know, being an, uh . . ." God she was uncomfortable, "a lesbian."

Elizabeth struggled with her own cup, catching it just as it knocked against the table, the contents covering her hand. She shot up quickly and was running her hand under cold water. "Henry, you can't just ask someone about their sexuality?" one of her wet hands was at her temple as if rubbing away an approaching headache, "I thought I'd raised you better than that?"

Rachel shrunk back down into her seat. There it was. The thing they'd been avoiding the entire evening. Both women had tried so hard for the boy between them, yet there it was, in the room now. Elizabeth had raised the child, proving to Rachel that she was only in the family home for the duration of his curiosity. After that she would be gone, forgotten about, occasionally they might mention her in passing but she wouldn't attend birthdays or Christmases. There would be no graduation or wedding invites. And that's how she'd wanted it, right? She'd given the boy to someone else that could offer him all that. One awkward meal in a cold farmhouse wouldn't—couldn't—change anything. Undo what had been done, rewrite their history.

"Rachel, I'm so sorry, I'll take you back to the station."

Elizabeth was clearly uncomfortable, Rachel neither knew nor cared why, she was just grateful to be leaving. Speeding along the inevitable.

They all knew she didn't have any answers to give the boy.

* * *

As she stepped out of the car, she was pulled back in by Elizabeth.

"It will get easier," she told her, letting go of her arm.

"Do you want it to?"

"I want my son to be happy."

For the second time today, Elizabeth's face was lit only by the mirror light. Before, when she had tried to prepare herself for the evening ahead, she had looked small and nervous, now Elizabeth just looked tired.

Rachel thought about all the ways she could possibly respond to that. Was this the portion of the evening that the forgotten meal had been leading to? Was this meant to be the part where Rachel explained her actions sixteen years ago, gave a trite justification for abandoning her child to a couple she had only met through words on paper—a couple that both her social worker, her unborn child's social worker, and Judi all agreed would be best fit for her son? *They're a great couple, lovely house in Kent. She's a business analyst, he's working on his PhD.*

All she could give the woman was half a smile.

"That's all any of us want."

She reached back for the door, relieved to see the lights of her train in the distance. She would have to run, so they would be spared from an awkward goodbye and an *until next time*.

There were more on her train this time, though she was left alone for her change at Ashford, where the coffee shop was closed, her only company a night worker changing the lining of the bins.

The automated voice read out the names of the stations, but she did not get off at Dover, she carried on through and pulled up the collar of her coat as she banged on Marc's door, and she watched more and more lights flick on as he approached.

He looked her up and down before opening the door wider and led her into his living room.

"Brother is in the spare room. You'll have to take the sofa."

She frowned at him before dropping onto her bed for the night.

"Half-brother," Marc clarified before leaving her and heading back up the stairs.

She figured Marc must be used to the routine now. Last time Rachel's stay had lasted nearly the entirety of Andy's eight-day fling with whatever-that-one's-name-was. She couldn't remember anything about him other than his size-ten worn navy Puma trainers that he'd left lying around the flat for her to trip over.

The first time Rachel had arrived on his doorstep in the middle of the night, Marc had sat her down, found her a beer and insisted they talk. He'd done the same the next time, but by the third time, he'd clearly resigned himself to the fact that this was simply how things were, how they would be. He told her that when he got married, when he and John—for his fictional husband was always called John—they would get a house with a lesbian annex for her over the garage. She would be able to host lesbian book club meetings, discuss moon cups while playing Tori Amos and whatever it was that lesbians do when they get together. "A descent of dykes," he'd called them before receiving a sharp smack on the shoulder and told not to use that word. She hated that word. *Dykes are Dutch dams. I'm a lesbian.*

Slumping down on the sofa, she checked her phone and found a couple of messages from Henry. The first was a thank you and an apology for the weirdness, the second was a suggestion that they meet at a Costa next time or a football game; he'd heard that Dover Athletic weren't terrible. She didn't know how to reply to him, or if she even wanted to, so she pushed them to the side. She turned off the light and rearranged her coat to sleep beneath it, not finding the energy to go to the airing cupboard and find some sheets.

In the darkness, she pretended she might be able to sleep.

Instead she thought about that afternoon on a sofa with Daniel, the irregularity of her period that meant she didn't notice until it was too late. She wondered about Daniel briefly, what he was doing now, if he ever thought about the time he lost his virginity to the girl who wanted a couple of hours off from being a lesbian, who just wanted to have a boyfriend like the rest of her friends, who wanted to try on heterosexuality and see if it could fit her too.

Rachel's thoughts moved to more enjoyable nights. Nights on various sofas with Andy, giggling like school girls, all of Andy's promises that this was definitely the last time as she came undone under Rachel's hands. She moved to the floor when she remembered the dying embers of Marc's house warming, the only two left still partying in the early hours. *Why are you kissing me? Because Marc Fucking Ward just bought a house. Because we're getting old.*

She suddenly hated that Andy had been in her life for so many years, that everything was tainted with her.

Henry

HE PUT THE remnants of his second favourite meal into Tupperware. Is it still Tupperware if it's an old Chinese container? Is a Hoover still a Hoover if it's a Dyson? Is he still a Cole if he's a King?

He washed up their plates. Henry had briefly thought about loading the dishwasher but wasn't sure what else he'd do with his time if he didn't wash up by hand. He didn't want to watch telly, his computer wasn't any fun all the time it was downstairs, and his Xbox seemed too trivial.

He didn't want to go online and be told that his goalkeeper was easier to score against than his mum. Which mum was the randomly assigned stranger on FIFA talking about? Was his birth mother easy? Is that why he'd been conceived? Was his adopted mother frigid? Is that why he didn't have her blood?

His mother walked back in as he was on to the drying up. She kissed him on the cheek and found a second tea towel. The dishes were put away in silence. He watched as she checked the temperature of the remains before putting them in the fridge. He wasn't sure if she knew that they probably wouldn't get eaten. That neither of them would have that meal again, its taste soured by the awkwardness of sharing it with Rachel, flavoured with unasked questions.

She followed him up the stairs, each allowing the other too much space as they passed in the hallway. They got ready for bed, the lights of the house slowly disappearing as they did the rounds.

When she told him goodnight, he didn't imagine she would be able to fall asleep any more than he suspected he would, but he shared her sentiments nonetheless.

Barely half an hour passed before he got back out of bed and found himself knocking on her door. Allowed in, he walked slowly to her bed and climbed under her covers. He was too old to be in her bed, but he didn't want to be old. He wanted to be small. He wanted to be—at the very least—six days younger than he was now.

He wanted to not have seen Rachel at the train station, he wanted not to have tracked her down and dragged her into their lives. He wanted his biggest worry to be if Sam was going to be in his life forever. If Sam was going to propose to his mum. If she would become a Turner and he would be the last Cole. If they would have a baby—could they have a baby? His mum wasn't that old. Or would they adopt? He could be the only Cole in a house of Turners. Would the new baby be a Turner if it had been a baby Something else before?

She wrapped her arm around him and pulled him closer to her.

"Have you spoken to Sam?"

She shook her head beside him.

"Do you want to?"

"Not particularly."

At a certain point in the night, his eyes always turned the world into a snowstorm, like a bad signal on an old analogue television. He had wanted to ask his science teacher about it, but he neither had the words to properly explain his question nor a science teacher to ask.

"Have you spoken to Rachel?" she asked him.

Her words pulled him out of his snowdrift. "No."

"I think I was wrong to invite her to the house."

"Like I was wrong to just turn up at her flat?"

"Different kind of wrong."

He could feel her frowning. She was probably trying to find the best words to explain.

"I think, perhaps, you need to meet somewhere neutral. Somewhere where you're not in her life, and she's not in yours. Somewhere where you can show her as much of Henry Alexander Cole as you wish to, and she can show you as much of Rachel King as she feels able."

"Do you think she has a middle name?"

"I don't know. We don't know who named her."

He leaned in closer now, he could feel one of her pulse points beating into his ear. "Do you think she ever gave me a name?"

When it became clear she wasn't going to answer the question (she would answer it in the morning, or in a couple of days. Drop it into a conversation in a week's time as if he had only just asked), when she left him back to the quiet of his snowstorm, he left her bed and retreated to his own. He put his television on and watched whatever channel had been on last. TVs didn't have snowstorms any more, it was all digital, the pictures just cracked into blocks of colours. There was a signer in the corner. Henry slowly drifted to sleep, the volume muted, watching the woman's hands tell a story he couldn't understand.

* * *

He was left to wake on his own. Glancing at his radio, he found it was nearly midday. He couldn't remember the last time he'd been allowed to sleep so late. He remembered it was an Isaac Weekend, so he should have been woken up hours ago by a four-year-old poking his face which happened whenever Isaac stayed over. He wondered how it would be explained to the small boy that he wouldn't be playing football in the big garden, as Isaac called it, with Henry this weekend. He wondered if Sam had a garden where he was staying or if Sam had spoken to his ex-wife to arrange another weekend. Maybe he had gone back to her. Maybe they would have another baby, a child that shared her colouring rather than a white one like Sam might have with his mother.

He stopped moving around and listened for the noises of the house. He couldn't hear the radio, so his mother wasn't in the kitchen below him; he couldn't hear the television, so she wasn't watching one of those Saturday morning magazine shows; and classical music wasn't playing, so she wasn't working in the study.

He checked his phone. No messages, so she hadn't left the house. Rachel hadn't replied either. The sudden realisation that he had two mothers caused a wave of nausea to hit.

Plenty of children had two mothers. In his year group alone, he was one of only a handful to have just one parent. Most seemed to have three or four. But now he had two again. He hadn't had two since he was eight months old. He had no memories of having two. He hadn't expected to have two again.

He found an old bottle of water beside his bed. The sip of liquid, now littered with bubbles where it had been abandoned for a couple of days, was enough to dispel it.

When he was younger, he made up stories about the things he and his dad did together. He repeated the stories so often to himself that it was hard to remember that it hadn't been his father who had first kicked a football to him. It had been a kid at school. His memories of his father were fictitious, fallacies forced into his head by the desire to be like everyone else, to have a mum *and* a dad.

He had two parents now, though. He had a mum, and he had a Rachel. He wondered if, should Rachel ever get married, he would have three mums.

He swapped his pyjamas for joggers and an old Arsenal shirt and headed downstairs.

He eventually found his mum sitting in the garden with a cup of coffee pressed tightly between her hands. Her eyes were closed, enjoying the last of the sun before it disappeared for its winter hibernation. His hands wrapped around his arms, goose bumps trying to warm him in the autumn breeze. She seemed unaffected by the chill.

"What do you want to do today?" she asked him, eyes still closed.

He shrugged before realising how futile his body language was. "Dunno."

"Have you completed all your homework?"

"Only just woken up," he sat down beside her and stole a sip of her drink, "give me a chance."

"Do you have much?"

"Not really, just have to copy up the notes I missed from Thursday. Anyway," he shrugged, "I've got all of half term."

He passed her back her coffee, but she waved him away. He would have preferred it with two sugars, actually, he would have preferred tea. Apparently, his dad had only drunk tea, his mother exclusively drank coffee, so he must have got the habit from him; but that seemed impossible, there was no DNA to link them, no predispositions to be passed along through blood. He wondered what Rachel drank. Maybe it was from her he'd acquired the taste.

He pulled out his mobile from his pocket and sent her another text. *Tea or coffee?*

Last year he'd come downstairs to find his mum and Sam sitting on the floor. She was leaning against the sofa, Sam was lying on his back staring up at the ceiling, hands cupping the back of his head, and both of them had been surrounded by newspapers. It was a Sunday, so they were swamped by all the supplements of the *The Observer*. Henry had walked away, not wanting to know why they were so happy.

He didn't like playing happy families. It was different when Isaac was around because that couldn't have been his life, there wouldn't have been a mix-raced child in the house had his dad lived. But when it was just Sam, when it was the three of them, he wondered if his life would have been like this all the time if his dad hadn't had the accident, if his dad hadn't been a sad man, if it was the childhood he didn't have.

They were still laughing when he'd walked back passed them to return to his room with his cup of tea. Curiosity got the better of him—as it often did—and he'd asked them what was going on.

His mum had cleared a space free of newspaper and had patted the spot next to her on the carpet.

"Come join us." She smiled at him. "We're falling in love."

Henry didn't understand.

"Aren't you in love already?"

"We thought so," Sam was sitting up now and poking about on the iPad, "but apparently there's more to it than we were led to believe." He slid the device along to him. "Take a look."

His mum had found an article about a new fad and thirty-six questions that lead to love. She'd read it to Sam and he'd ended up Googling the study. They had spent the last twenty minutes in hysterics at either the questions or the answers one of them had offered.

Henry remembered it vividly, as he could an annoyingly large number of things. Like every conversation with Alyssa Finch that had led up to his touching her breast. *Left. Above bra, below shirt. Hardened nipple.* That had been a Sunday too. His memory had been a blessing while he was revising for his GCSEs, but sometimes it was just annoying. Like remembering, in near perfect detail, the first time he had seen his mum cry sad tears because he had come home at eleven with questions about Grace.

He wondered what Grace was doing now; she hadn't come back for her A Levels.

Both turned to his phone as it beeped Rachel's reply. *Coffee. Why?* His mum looked at him weirdly as she, too, read the message across his locked screen.

"I wondered if I like tea because she likes tea."

"I think you like tea because, despite my protestations, my warnings about hot drinks and statistics about burns on babies, most of the time your father held you he was also holding a cup of tea."

She was smiling. "On the rare occasions he wasn't holding a cup of tea, his breath stank of the stuff." Henry was smiling too now. "Used to drive me mad. For the first year we were together I wouldn't let him near me without a Tic Tac first."

"Why only a year?"

"I was spending too much of my student grant on mints."

He stood up and headed into the kitchen. As the kettle boiled, she put her cup down beside it, a silent instruction that he was to make her a drink too.

"Can you remember any of those questions you and Sam 'fell in love' to?"

She probably hadn't seen his air quotes as her head was in the fridge looking for lunch. He noticed the Tupperware was ignored in place of bread and eggs. "What?"

"I was thinking some of them could be useful to get to know Rachel."

"One was about whether you look in your tissue after you blow your nose." She inspected the egg carton, he assumed her to be reading the expiration date. "But I think that one might have been from the parody article I read in the paper."

"You seem happier this morning," he said as he handed across her coffee.

Elizabeth

SHE DIDN'T KNOW when she'd eventually managed to fall asleep. She figured it was at least a couple of hours after Henry's departure from her bed. But she knew it was a text that eventually woke her on Saturday morning:

So, I've just walked in on your boyfriend on the toilet.

It was followed quickly by, Does he know about me? He saw me at the train station. What do you want me to say? The third read, NOW WOULD BE GOOD!!!!

She instinctively rubbed her eyes and looked at the messages from Rachel again. Once they were processed, she tried to summon up the energy to be angry with Sam for telling her that he was at his brother's, when he was clearly finding girls in their twenties to sleep with. But she found any attempts at anger were quickly displaced by questioning the literal meaning of his words.

He had told her he was staying at his brother's on Thursday. She suddenly couldn't remember if he said he would remain there. Was it a lie? Was it infidelity? She wasn't being intimate with him—she wasn't allowing him into her life fully—why should he commit to just her alone?

Her final question to herself was if she was actually surprised. He had moved from his wife, twenty-eight when the divorce papers came through, to her, thirty-nine when they'd crossed paths in the car park. Furthermore, their relationship had moved at a snail's pace; he had constantly been telling her he wanted more than she was offering. Perhaps he had found in another younger woman something that she was unwilling to give.

After three years, what did they really have to show for their time together? Did either of them actually owe the other anything?

Her phone screen was illuminated again. A picture of Sam holding a much smaller Isaac was displayed. Isaac was reaching for the phone, apparently intrigued by the plastic object taking his photo. Henry must have set it when he was feeling happier about Sam being in their lives. She let the phone ring until the picture disappeared.

She wouldn't have thought Andrea was his type. Then again, maybe she was just his type, with her dark skin like that of Mariel's, like that of his son's. Perhaps it was she who wasn't his type; too old, too English, too ordinary. Mariel always looked as if she held within her all the mysteries of the world, and Elizabeth got the impression, from their brief encounter, that Andrea would spill every secret without a moment's hesitation. Perhaps that was her appeal; Andrea left no unanswered questions, whereas Elizabeth refused to acknowledge he'd even asked any.

A fresh text message brought her back to her bed, to the phone in her hand. The woman Henry accosted in London just found me with my trousers down. I refuse to believe this is a coincidence. Will you please tell me what's going on?

No kisses closed his demand, no terms of endearment bookended his message. There was no indication that he'd spent the night with another woman.

She looked at the time, big and bold in the centre of her lock screen, overshadowing his cold message. It wasn't even eight yet. She threw off her covers, traded their warmth for that of her dressing gown, and proceeded to run a bath. She left the water to itself and made a cup of coffee, stepping quietly around the house so as not to disturb Henry, found her book in the living room and headed back upstairs with it and her drink.

She slipped into the bath, knowing the book wouldn't be read and her coffee would probably lie forgotten. Instead she thought about Sam's hands tracing over Andrea's body, his mouth against hers. She wondered if he touched Andrea as he had touched her. Andrea didn't have as much of a chest as she did, maybe he hadn't paid as much attention to it as he usually did hers. Maybe he didn't bother with foreplay at all. Maybe it was quick and animalistic, raw with passion. It had always been quiet between them for fear of disturbing Henry. Fearing interruption, their encounters were often swift and to the point. Perhaps that was why he had sped so soon to another—he sought out something he'd been missing—he wanted to be loud and unrestrained, he wanted to go all night and have a woman scream for him, not worry about a teenager overhearing.

Her thoughts moved to Rachel who would have lain in the next room. Had she heard them? Wondered about the man causing all the noise? Maybe she'd got back late and they'd already finished. Sam had a tendency to fall asleep almost as soon as he'd tied the end of the condom, or maybe it was just her—she simply didn't have what it took to keep him awake.

Feeling neither soothed nor cleansed, she let the water run out and dried herself. After putting on her clothes for the day she looked back to her phone, ignoring the message from Sam and went back to the latest three from Rachel. This wasn't her fault, she wasn't to choose who her flat mate took to bed with her.

"Too late," Rachel answered her call.

"What did you say?"

"Nothing. I just grabbed my coat and left."

"Sorry he forced you out of your own home."

"What? No, I was at Mark's last night." There was a pause. "I had planned to stay in his spare room, but apparently your—"

"Sam."

"Sam was in it. I had to settle for the sofa."

Elizabeth felt foolish for wasting so much time thinking about

Andrea, stupid at her hasty assumption. However, the relief that Sam hadn't been unfaithful didn't follow. Infidelity would have made so many decisions for her. She could have played the indignant partner, given him an actual reason for leaving. Instead she was back to where she was before she'd been woken—she had a man living in her house who wasn't talking to her and choices still had to be made.

"Why didn't you go home last night?"

"Andy and I . . ."

"Yeah," she breathed, sensing there was no end to her sentence in sight, "I think Sam and I are in a similar place."

"You mean you think you're in love with him, he's giving you just enough to keep you but not enough to make you think he'll give up others for thoroughly mundane monogamy?"

"Okay, maybe not that similar." Elizabeth smiled despite herself.

"Why is Sam staying with Mark? You guys looked like the picture-perfect family when I saw you in London. Your conversation on the train could have come straight out of 2point4 Children." Rachel sounded just like Henry when she compared real life to film and television.

"I haven't told him where we were on Wednesday. I haven't told him that Henry's adopted."

"I know how you feel, I hadn't told Andy either."

"How did she take it?"

"Amazingly," Rachel said through a sigh.

Elizabeth heard noises that she couldn't place coming through the phone. Trying to picture Rachel as they were speaking, she couldn't make the background sound fit the image she was creating.

"Where are you?"

"Deal beach."

Suddenly she could hear waves crashing, as if they had been waiting for permission to enter the conversation too.

"Could you hear me playing with the pebbles?"

Elizabeth was about to answer when realization dawned like a new day. "Mark . . ." She put the pieces together. "Marc. Marcus. Marcus moved to Deal about six months ago."

"Yeah."

"Had a housewarming and pompously called it a Death Pledge Party."

"Yeah, Andy and I considered going in togas."

"We went to that party; Sam insisted on buying him this god-awful lamp."

Their world was seemingly so small, they should have met by now, it shouldn't have fallen to a chance encounter outside some grubby toilets at a station in London. It made no sense.

"I didn't see you there."

"We, uh, we came late." Rachel's voice was soft yet sounded full of sadness.

"You okay?"

"Just remembering why we were late."

She could see Rachel on the beach now. She was sitting facing the sea, to the right of the pier near the Old Timeball Tower. The double buttons of her coat were undone, showing the blue shirt she had been wearing the night before, her hair in a messy pony tail with loose sections cutting across her face in the breeze. Rachel's left hand would be subconsciously fiddling with the pebbles of the beach, picking them up just to drop them back down, the salt water residue starting to dry her skin. Her right was holding the phone to her ear, holding Elizabeth's voice close to her.

"Sam called you 'the woman Henry accosted' when he texted me."

"I wouldn't say the kid 'accosted' me. I had been staring at him for, like, five minutes. Not sure I even blinked. If a stranger had looked at me like that when I was a kid, I would have done far more than 'accost', and I certainly wouldn't have been as polite about it." She laughed gently. Pebbles continued to clack against each other.

"How did you know who he was? You hadn't seen a picture in

years."

The laughter stopped; just the clacking of pebbles and the crashing of the waves remained. "I didn't. It wasn't until he got off the train did I realise who he was. Should have realised earlier, he looks just like his father did at that age."

"Who—"

"Don't," Rachel's voice was hard now. "Ask me anything else. Anything and I will answer. Just not that."

The silence was ever growing around them, sucking them in like entropy; if Elizabeth didn't stop it soon, she assumed Rachel would leave and find shelter.

"Henry wanted to know if you ever named him."

"If I'd given him a name, we wouldn't be speaking. From your first letter he's been Henry Alexander Cole. And if he doesn't like that answer—" Rachel's tone shifted back to the lightness it had been before. "Remind him I was seventeen and he'll be glad I didn't. If left to me he would have received some unisex name based on whichever actress I fancied at the time."

She didn't know how or when she'd stepped into the garden, but when the phone call ended—Battery dying. Should go home at some point—that was where she found herself. The October sun, while hardly warm, was enough to make her bask and she wondered if the sun was shining on Rachel.

"What do you want to do today?" she asked as she heard Henry approach. She was still looking at the phone nestled between her hands.

"Dunno."

"Have you completed all your homework?"

"Only just woken up."

She felt him sit beside her, taking the cup she didn't remember rescuing from the bathroom from her hand.

"Give me a chance."

"Do you have much?"

"Not really, just have to copy up the notes I missed from Thursday. Anyway, I've got all of half term."

They were in the kitchen when Henry started asking obscure, even by his own esoteric standards, questions.

He'd made her a fresh cup of coffee as she rummaged through the fridge, bypassing the leftover meal from last night, looking for something to eat. He tentatively asked her about when she fell in love with Sam. She busied herself with the task, not wanting to analyse—to really consider—if she had fallen in love with him. She worried that she'd simply fallen for complacency, fallen for an easy life with an easy man. She shook her head of thoughts of him, looking to the eggs for answers of what to eat rather than answers of what to do about the man whose possessions remained in her house.

"What?" she eventually replied, realising that Henry was waiting as he would continue to wait until his question was answered.

"I was thinking some of them could be useful to get to know Rachel."

Then there it was, nestled between the cheese and a rather sad looking onion was the memory of what Henry was referring to. There had been a stupid article in The Observer months ago. Sam had found it hilarious, made her read out the questions as he would answer in a gradually thickening American accent, his responses getting more ridiculous as her patience with his game waned.

"One was about whether you look in your tissue after you blow your nose." She inspected the eggs for a date. "But I think that one might have been from the parody article I read in the paper."

"You seem happier this morning," he told her as he passed her coffee.

She thought about his comment. Was she any happier? And happier than what? She brushed his words aside and focused her thoughts on the fridge.

"I think we've got enough fresh vegetables for frittata; will you eat with me?"

Henry moved to sit on one of the breakfast bar stools, turning his cup in his hands, he'd nodded his reply to her offer of lunch but clearly had more on his mind.

"Ask it." She told him as she started cutting potatoes.

"Did Sam leave, or did you kick him out?"

"He decided to stay with his brother for a couple of nights."

"Why?"

"He had some questions that I didn't want to answer. He got annoyed and told me I wasn't ready to live with him."

"You seem happier without him in the house."

"As do you." She tipped the potatoes into a pan and fiddled with the gas.

"Caitlin says you like Isaac more than Sam." He'd pulled an onion towards him and started peeling at the layers.

"Caitlin says too much."

"Mum." He drew out the word the same way he did when he wanted to borrow money, or stay out late on a school night.

"Henry?"

"Have you ever been with a woman?"

Henry had always asked a lot of questions. She suspected Henry always would.

Why does England have a queen?

Why do dogs have four legs, but we only have two?

Why aren't there dinosaurs anymore?

Why doesn't Daddy live with us?

Why did you adopt me?

What was I called before I was called Henry Alexander Cole?

Every single one of his questions received an answer. If she didn't know it, she would sit him on her lap, a book placed on his own, and read the answer with him, their encyclopaedia the most worn of all their books, thumbed through and dog eared, the section on kings and queens the patchiest of all the pages.

Having a king or queen is a type of government. We call that a monarchy. But our queen, the British queen, is more a figure head now; meaning that she doesn't make or pass laws, we elect people to do that. Like the people Michael works with.

Dogs' backs are different to ours, they need four legs help them balance. Like a table. We only need two legs because we evolved differently. We're similar to monkeys. You've seen how monkeys walk.

Scientists found a big hole. They think an asteroid—that's a rock falling from space—hit the Earth and that killed all the dinosaurs. There would have been earthquakes, fires, tsunamis and lots and lots of dust in the air making it difficult for them to breathe. The dinosaurs wouldn't have been able to survive.

Your father was in a car crash, you were very small, you still needed to be carried everywhere. Your father would live with us if he could, he doted on you very much and he would have loved to see the man you're becoming.

Your father and I, before we had even married, always knew we wanted a little man in our home. I always knew he would be called Henry Alexander Cole. A couple of years after we married, we decided we were ready for our little man and to call him Henry Alexander Cole. We spoke to lots of different people, they found a young woman with a tiny baby growing inside her tummy. She didn't think she could love you as much as your father and I could love you. We wrote her letters, Grandma Clara and Grandpa Henry wrote one, Caitlin even wrote to her. This young woman just wanted for you to be loved, and she chose your father and I to love you. And you are loved very much. You are the most loved little man in all the world.

You've always been called Henry Alexander Cole—

No, before. When I was a baby growing in a tummy—

You were called baby King. But I always knew you would be called Henry Alexander Cole, just as I always knew I would dote on you.

Yet this was a question far out of her reach. She schooled her features and returned her attention to the eggs. "Caitlin says too much," was all she could offer in reply.

Rachel

SHE WAS HUGGING her knees, looking out at the sea. A sensible person would have gone inside by now, the grey sky and greyer sea before her reminding her that a British autumn is a miserable affair. Cold and bleak, like a Dickensian novel.

She was too tired for this. Too tired to fend off the cold and the maudlin thoughts pinning her to the beach.

She should have gone home last night, should have slept in her bed and perhaps she could still be there now. Andy would have popped her head in, brought her a cup of coffee and bounced on the bed, trying to pull her out of it. Insist they do something with the day. *Let's go on an adventure.*

But adventuring with Andy wasn't getting her anywhere. Andy would always need more, determined to be something—*anything*—other than average. Ironic considering that average was all that Rachel had ever wanted to be. That desire to be like everybody else, even for ten minutes, had led her to this moment.

She would never be enough for Andy, making her just another last on a long list of unattainable women that Rachel had fallen for.

Marc, during one of her longer stays with him, had tried to—tentatively, ever so tentatively, after buttering her up with a roast dinner and some expensive red wine—suggest that perhaps it was because a life in foster care had given her a fear of rejection. By falling for women she could never be with, constructing entire relationships in her head alone, she would never be turned away.

Rachel had quickly headed back to the flat and spent an insufferable weekend with Andy and who-ever-that-one-was.

She had considered Marc's words, several times in fact. Once she had taken him out to dinner—one of many owed for all the nights staying at his—and explained to him at length why his theorem, while it could apply to many who'd grown up in care, couldn't apply to her.

She had always been incredibly fortunate with her placements. The first home she remembered living in she stayed until she was seven. It had been a three-bedroomed detached house on the outskirts of Harlow, with two wonderful adults, a Shih Tzu and a whole host of other children that came and went from the third and fourth bedrooms. But then they moved to Spain wishing to spend their retirement in the sun, they'd told her that she would have gone too but the law wouldn't allow, so she had to stay in Essex. They had sent her Christmas and birthday cards for a couple of years, she had kept the exotic Spanish stamps in a box by her bed with a picture of her holding Sheila the Shih Tzu.

Tony and Debbie had helped the transition to an almost identical house with a slightly younger couple: he was a teacher at a secondary school in Epping, she hadn't worked since having their boys, but the twins were at university now and Rachel, as a 'long term placement,' would fill the empty nest.

When she was nine, with the boys home for Christmas, the family had sat her down and told her that she could call them Mum and Dad as she'd unwrapped a Tottenham Hotspurs' shirt with *Milner 9* on the back.

But Rachel had a Mum and Dad and she didn't know where they were, then there had been Debbie and Tony, they had been called Mum and Dad too, but they had moved to Spain. She didn't want another Mum and Dad. If she called them Mum and Dad they might go away.

With Judi, she would watch *ER* and dream of a life with Carol

Hathaway, it was Judi that accompanied her to her ultrasounds and it was Judi that had almost had her hand broken during the birth. It was Robert who had 'always had an inkling' she was gay. It was Robert, when she left for university, who had whispered in her ear that they would have adopted her properly if they could have. It was Judi and Robert who had loved her regardless of everything.

Rachel was loved, she had family, it was a fear of rejection from them that accounted for a great many things in her life, but it wasn't a fear of rejection that meant she kept falling for unattainable women, so Marc's theory didn't apply to her. Her attachment to Andrea Grigoriadis was based on something else.

"Then what is it?" he'd asked, a fork of steak poised by his lips, "because I've overheard you two, too many times now, and Andy doesn't sound that good."

Rachel had picked apart her pretentious little burger with a brioche bun and shrugged her shoulders. Firefly thoughts flew around her head, and as one answer reached the top, another would glow brighter. Unable to find the perfect words, she popped a sweet potato fry in her mouth and gave him another shrug.

Her theory was that she spent too long in her head, that the tangible world around her could never measure up to the universe she had created in her mind. She didn't have the words to articulate this to him fully though. Marc would never understand the conflict of battling realities, of hoping her imaginary world would one day conquer the actual, that it was better to do nothing and hope, than to follow through and fail.

She threw one last pebble towards the sea, it didn't quite reach the water but caused a ripple effect of rocks so one eventually met the incoming tide and looked at her phone for the time. Pressing the home screen, a sad-looking red battery told her that the message back to Henry had been the last straw. She looked at her watch instead; it was almost three. Had her phone battery lasted, she would be receiving messages from Luke of score predictions and questions about changes to her fantasy football team. She stretched out her legs and slowly stood, her lower half trying to acclimatise to no longer having to mould around the stony beach, before slowly meandering back to the train station.

This is a Southeastern service to London St Pancras, calling at Walmer, Martin Mill, Dover Priory, Folkestone Central, Folkestone West, Ashford International, Ebbsfleet International, Stratford International and London St Pancras International Station.

The station was quiet, no guards could be seen. She instinctively checked her phone for the time, the sad red battery reminding her why she wasn't listening to music, before going to her watch. It was after five now, so there would be more messages from Luke either bragging or despairing about his predictions and how much he had won or lost from his accumulator at the bookies. *Don't tell dad xx* the messages always ended, despite the fact he was forty-four and had a family of his own. *Will tell Imogen though xx* was always her reply; he would be waiting for it.

She rearranged her jacket, pushed her hands in her pockets, started her walk and hoped she could remember the way.

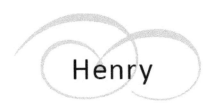

Henry

HE HAD BEEN on the computer when Sam finally returned, working on his homework as *Final Score* played on the telly. His mum had looked up from her book, clearly as startled by Sam's presence as he was. She'd told him to keep working as she put her slippers back on and headed out to the dining room, careful to shut the door behind her. Their conversation, instantly becoming a muffled argument, grew louder before disappearing completely.

Henry muted the television but still couldn't hear their voices. He saved his work and headed over to the door, but still there was nothing.

She must have taken Sam into the kitchen, be making him a drink, trying to appease him. Him mum didn't do that though, she had never used drinks to calm him down when he was upset; it was always soothing touches, words of encouragement to coax relaxation, kisses on bruised knees to make them better, promises that it would all be all right.

Besides, the kitchen was where she went to relax, she liked to cook elaborate meals, to bake cakes like her father had taught her with either Radio 4 or 6 Music playing in the background. She wouldn't take an argument in there, fearful of tainting her sacred kitchen with angry words.

He opened the door a crack and expected to see them sitting either side of the dining room table. Her arms would be folded tightly across her chest, Sam's fingers would be splayed out on the table in front of him, silence biting between them as they both thought about the words about to be exchanged. But the room was empty, the rough sawn oak left bare, save from Isaac's stray dinosaur lying on its side.

Henry had never thought of his mum's taste in furniture as imposing before, but looking at the big, dark, wooden table he was suddenly glad the awkward meal with Rachel had been held in the kitchen. The furniture in the house had been the same for as long as he could remember; the living room sofa had changed and the technology around the house updated, but aside from that the furnishings had, largely, remained the static. He suddenly realised why: she would have picked it out with his dad when they'd first moved in. It might not have been to her taste at all, it might have been what he would have wanted, or a pleading compromise made in *Habitat*.

It was only now, as Henry followed the sounds of the suppressed argument around the downstairs of the house, that he realised the ghost of his father sat heavy on his mother's shoulders as well as his own. That his father joined them for every meal and lay beside her each night. The bed she shared with Sam, cramped with his father squashed between them.

No wonder she never truly looked happy when Sam was in the room.

Henry found their argument taking place in the final downstairs room, where he should have expected it to be all the while. The study was his mother's kingdom, and if a battle were to be had, of course she'd draw him into her office; she'd sit behind her desk (or was it his father's desk? He had been working on his PhD when he had his accident), oak with a dark varnish dark like the table in the dining room, and wait for Sam to falter and lay his own fate at her feet.

The door was closed, just a little crack of light emanating from beneath it, but he could hear Sam. He was pacing, his footsteps sounding like drum beats in the quiet of the room. And then the first shot of the war rang out:

"Who is she?"

"Sam—"

"Do not try and plicate me, I am not a child."

Sam was a quiet man, Henry had never heard him raise his voice, but his enunciation was so crisp, so precise that simple word would have been able to bring an army to its knees.

"Our relationship is dying, Elizabeth."

"It was before Rachel arrived and it will be afterwards."

Henry could listen no more.

This was Sam's Somme and he was marching slowly to his death.

Henry withdrew, his intention to switch *Final Score* for the radio and listen to coverage of the late kick off. Arsenal were playing away at Stamford Bridge, so if he was really lucky, he would be able to find somebody streaming the game online.

But then the door knocker sounded.

"Rachel." He looked around quickly, before pulling the porch door to, and standing in the doorway, his arms folded across his chest. "You shouldn't be here."

"I would have called but—" He watched as she removed her phone from her jeans, the same jeans she'd worn last night, and presented her dead battery. He shook his head and pointed behind her to Sam's beaten old Land Rover next to his mum's pristine Audi. "Sam's here?" He nodded. "How bad is it?"

"I stopped listening when he started talking about palliative care." He shrugged and let his words tail away.

"I shouldn't have come. I'm sorry."

Suddenly she was turning back, retreating as Sam should have done before her, and yet Henry's hand shot out and pulled her back. They were all in No Man's Land because he'd sought her out, dragged her—kicking and screaming—into their lives, he believed her to have the answers, he had to keep hold of that belief.

"You don't have to." He looked back to the second door, but he wasn't really expecting either his mum or Sam to emerge.

Rachel obediently followed him into the kitchen, standing self-consciously as he put the kettle on to boil. He fussed around with cups and teaspoons before he realised he didn't actually know what he was doing.

"How do you take your coffee?"

"Black and one." She remained rigid, her eyes darting around the room as if checking for danger.

"You should probably sit down, pretend this isn't weird as . . ." He stopped himself before he swore; he wasn't sure if he should do that in front of Rachel. "We're here now. I chased you down. Brought you here. We need to figure out what happens next."

"The secret's out," she mused, looking across at the chair she'd sat less than twenty-four hours previously, "then why are your mum and Sam fighting?"

"Because she decided staying with Sam was better than loneliness."

"I don't get you, kid." Her hands were at her temples as his mum's often were after a long day. "How can you go from Sheldon Cooper to Oprah in a couple of sentences?"

"Who's Oprah?"

"And that's how old I am, I make cultural references that are no longer relevant."

She kicked off her trainers and shrugged off her coat, hanging it on the chair she'd sat at the night before, and headed to the small, worn leather sofa in the corner, tucking her legs beneath her as she sat.

He shook his head, not quite sure what to do with that information. "What's your favourite film?" he asked instead, passing her the cup of coffee as he sat down opposite her.

"There are too many, you can't ask someone to pick just one. Besides," she blew on her drink causing ripples to cross the small black pond, "in what situation am I going to have to watch just one film for the rest of my life? I get stranded on a desert island with a TV and DVD player?"

"I suppose."

He thought of Kirsty Young and *Desert Island Discs*. His mum always had that programme on as she prepared lunch on a Sunday, it had never occurred to him how stupid the premise was. Perhaps the discs were vinyl, the record player a wind-up gramophone.

He pictured himself on a desert island, he wasn't sure if he would be Tom Hanks or Matthew Fox, if he'd have a volleyball for company or if he would be trapped in some metaphorical purgatory. Maybe that's what these past few days had been, the awkwardness and the pain that engulfed them all. Maybe if he'd paid more attention in his RE lessons he would know.

Henry let his own drink warm his hands. Despite the fact that the house was perpetually cold, it never occurred to him to don more layers, it was just part of the way things are.

"Why are you here?" Regardless of the softness to his voice, he knew the words were harsh.

Rachel took another sip of her coffee before: "I wanted to speak with your mum."

"You should have called."

"Phone's dead, remember?" He looked across at her, all of her clothes were the same. "I didn't go home last night," she explained as if she'd heard his unvoiced question. "That's why they're fighting, I walked in on Sam on the loo."

"I don't understand."

"How long have your mum and Sam been together?"

"She met him when I was thirteen." He watched as she let out a silent laugh. It barely touched her lips, if it hadn't been for the slight roll of her shoulders there would be no indication it had happened. "What?"

"Of all the ways to meet each other, it shouldn't have been at a train station."

He was on his feet so quickly that his drink spilled over the edge of his cup, leaving a trail of tea down the light grey of his jogging bottoms.

"Fuck!"

"It's all right, kid, it's just tea."

That wasn't why he was annoyed though.

"Why do adults always do this?" He was articulating wildly with his hands, spilling more of his tea in his wake. "You never say what you actually want to say, you say anything but. Like you're all politicians. Analysts are being paid hundreds of pounds to work out why people are voting anti-establishment—they're not, they're voting for people that say what's on their mind." He turned to face her and saw her shoulders gently rocking. "Why are you laughing at me?"

"I'm not laughing *at* you." Rachel was on her feet too now, her coffee cup resting on the counter top, her arm outstretched as if she was about to reach for his. It never touched him though. "What do you want to know?"

"And you'll answer? Properly, like a teacher not Theresa May?"

She nodded. "To the best of my ability."

He leaned back against the counter, his arms folded tightly across his chest, face contorted into a tight frown. "You walked in on Sam on the loo?"

"My best friend, Mark, is his half-brother. I stayed at his last night, so did Sam. Mark doesn't have a lock on his bathroom door."

"Mark as in Marcus?"

She nodded, sitting back down, tucking her feet under her again so she was sitting on her ankles like his mother did.

"Why didn't you go home?"

"I didn't want to face Andy."

"Because of me?"

"No, because of me." That answer didn't satisfy him though,

138

something that must have been evident across his features as she pressed on. "Our relationship is complicated, and I have this sudden urge to make it uncomplicated."

"Because she's not gay?"

"Because she's not very good at monogamy. You know what that means?"

"One man, one woman." He caught the roll of her eyes.

Alyssa, as the only black pupil in sixth from, often told him to check his privilege, that he needed to be 'woke'. He wasn't quite sure what that meant, but he knew it had something to do with being white, male and heterosexual. She sometimes mentioned cis-gendered, but he *really* didn't know what that meant.

"Sorry. One person, one *other* person," he corrected before pushing onto his next question: "Have you always been a lesbian?"

"Not that I've always understood what that meant, but yes."

"But you got pregnant?"

"I got pregnant."

She stretched out for her coffee, unable to quite reach it he passed it down to her, before settling at one of the seats around the table.

"I've not always been as secure in who I am as I am now."

Henry was frowning again.

"Look." She leaned forward. "Do you know the kind of person you want to be for the rest of your life?"

"I don't think I know the kind of person I want to be tomorrow."

They filled the silence between them by pretending it wasn't there; they sipped at their drinks and he suddenly found the brown tea staining his trousers more fascinating than it should have been. He wondered if that could be the colour of sand on his desert island; he thought about who he'd want to rescue him. He thought about his mum. His mums.

This Rachel was so different from the Rachel he'd met before. The first one had been quiet, almost afraid to speak. The second, the one that looked just like this one—same jeans, same blue shirt, same hair (albeit slightly cleaner) in a messy pony tail—had been painfully polite, afraid to put a foot wrong. This one though, this Rachel, the Rachel sitting before him in his kitchen, drinking out of his Arsenal mug without complaint, despite her preference for Spurs, the Rachel with her shoes off and a toe poking out of a hole in her socks, revealing a painted nail—navy, slightly chipped—this Rachel seemed to be emboldened with the type of confidence that had led him to track her down in the first instance.

"Do you regret it?"

Elizabeth

SAM HAD FINALLY stopped pacing and was sitting on the Chesterfield beneath the window. She watched him as he folded his arms and crossed his legs, trying to make himself tall in his seat, raise himself up after she'd laughed in his face.

It said so much about the pair of them that just as she was willing to admit to the failing of another relationship, Sam was adamant he was going to save it. At the moment it was working, but it seemed so superficial. Too practised, too precise. An affair would give one of them a reason to call it time on this production. Elizabeth suddenly wished Sam was sleeping with Andrea. It would simply be so much easier for the pair of them; there would be a tangible reason for their end.

"I think Henry and I will go to my parents' for a couple of days, I think it would be best if you pack up your things while we're away."

"And what I think?"

"It doesn't matter, if we're not thinking the same."

She watched him open his mouth, only to promptly close it again. She watched him swallow whatever words were forming on his tongue. He sat up straighter, uncrossed his arms just to cross them tighter again. He separated his legs and unfolded his arms once more. His right hand went to the back of his neck and scratched at the mole just below his hair line. Had he been wearing his glasses she guessed he would have started to clean them on his shirt. He was fidgeting, playing for time, but the seconds were trickling through the space between them; he only had his hands, there was no way he could stop the shifting sands.

Finally, he stood.

"Will you always love Alex more?" Sam asked quietly, a stolen glance to a black and white photo of a man staring down at Edinburgh from Arthur's Seat, wind playing with his hair.

Elizabeth had been asked that question before. It was a lifetime ago and came from a different set of lips. Just as had no answer then, she found she didn't have an answer now.

The last grain of sand had reached the bottom of their hourglass, Sam was gone and she was no closer to finding a response. What she did realise though, as she heard the heavy sound of his diesel engine pull away from her house, now that all the sand was in the bottom bulb, she was no longer battling the waves she couldn't hold back.

She was Canute in her throne as the sea laughed at her powerlessness.

She tipped back in her chair, her feet on the edge of the table and a small smile danced across her lips. She let it play there for a time, let it have its moment, before slipping out of her chair and leaving her study behind her. She would sweep up the sand another time, for now she would talk to Henry about spending his half term with his grandparents; it wasn't too cold, he could go camping with his grandfather while she could listen to her mother explain that she'd never liked Sam anyway. Her mother would tell her all about a nice divorcé that had just moved to the village and started attending the church. She would sit and listen to her mother ramble on and on about him, the house this man had moved into (*on the market for months, you know the one I mean, next to the Joneses', lovely garden but it needs a lot of work on the inside*), and he would have a Beagle or a Labrador, and he would look like Colin Firth or Hugh Bonneville. She would think of Rachel the entire time.

She shook her head, unsure of where that last thought had come from. She glanced down at her phone, pressing the home screen, it displayed only the time—nearing six now—no new messages, though she expected a phone call from Caitlin later, wanting to know how last night's dinner had gone.

She rose from her seat and went in search of Henry, perhaps he had heard from Rachel, maybe they had continued to talk about tea verses coffee, about favourite colours, books and films.

She found the house oddly quiet. Usually there was some kind of background noise, if not the television, the radio. She'd left Henry watching *Final Score,* and, as she hadn't returned, she knew he would be trying to find the late game illegally, streaming online somewhere. But she heard nothing as she approached the living room, not even the sounds of him softly cursing their internet provider. She opened the living room door, it was *Pointless* now, Alexander Armstrong and Richard Osman silently quipping at each other on the muted television, the computer's screensaver scrolling through old photographs.

She headed back across the dining room and to the kitchen, the palm of her hand against the wood of its door before she heard anything other than her own thoughts.

"Do you regret it?" Elizabeth heard her son ask.

She retracted her hand from door with such speed, as if it had burnt her. Her fingers balled quickly into her palms, pressing crescents into them, her nails bending slightly under the pressure of meeting her skin.

"Kid . . ." came Rachel's slow reply.

Elizabeth's middle finger slipped along her thumb, its nail grating against the soft skin of her print. Caitlin told her that this habit made her look like she was lacking the confidence to click her fingers. Her mother had always said that the compulsion would irritate her skin. Alex had always taken her hand when she got into this fixation, entwined his fingers with hers and squeezed them between his own. Sam hadn't noticed she'd been doing it the first time he'd told her he loved her.

"You're asking the wrong question," Rachel tried again after what seemed like an eternity of silence.

"What should I be asking then?"

Elizabeth leant against the wall, her back to their conversation, her finger still stuttering against her thumb, her heart pounding deep in her chest.

"You went all kinds of Edward Snowden tracking down my parents, but I've always had access to my paperwork. All I had to do was ask my social worker."

"Why didn't you?"

"Because what if I was the reason?"

The house was silent again, the only sound coming from the steady scraping of her skin between her middle finger and thumb.

Elizabeth closed her eyes and pictured Henry and Rachel in her kitchen. He was sitting on a counter top, she was leaning against the island. Her hands were gripping the marble, knuckles whitening as she held on tighter. His brows knitted into a frown.

"Maybe I'd cried too much as a baby. Maybe my hair was the wrong colour. Maybe they didn't like this weird birth mark I have on my left side." Elizabeth shouldn't be listening to this conversation, but she didn't move from the wall. "A little after my seventeenth birthday I realised they probably had their reasons."

"What happened?"

"I found out there was this tiny, well I guess you weren't so tiny by that point, thing growing inside me."

"Thing?"

"Thing."

Elizabeth's thumb was sore now. She switched from the middle finger on her right hand, to the index finger on her left. This nail was a little more worn, it caught on her skin.

"There was freezing jelly on my stomach, a black and white image on a screen that looked like nothing I could explain, but there was a heartbeat. It was so strong, so fast, like a runner beating down on a pavement. The nurse said I was probably about twenty-five weeks. And I realised then that I didn't need to know, *want* to know, why my parents put me into care, because I had to do the same."

"Why did you come here today?"

"I told you, I want to speak to your mum."

Elizabeth pushed herself away from the wall and swiped at her eyes. She glanced at her palm which was streaked with the black of her mascara. She climbed the stairs two at a time, quickly to get into the bathroom and wash her face, reapply her makeup. Once done, she ran her wrists under the cold tap and tried to steady her heartrate.

She looked in the mirror and practised what she was going to say. It was getting late, too late to cook, they could order a takeaway. Henry had an app for that, he could have a look to see what he wanted to eat. She would feign surprise at finding Rachel in her kitchen, quickly compose herself and would invite her for supper if Rachel wanted to stay.

Elizabeth went back down the stairs, careful to make noise, determinedly stepping on the bottom to last stair knowing that it creaked. She didn't want to surprise them, she wanted them to hear her coming, to give them an opportunity to close their conversation.

"Do you fancy a takeaway?" she asked Henry as she pushed through the door, "I can't be bothered to cook. What was that Indian we liked?"

She stopped and made sure to look shocked at the woman sitting on her sofa. "Rachel?"

"Hi." The woman held up her hand, a half-hearted wave to match the lacklustre greeting.

"What are you doing here?"

"She wants to talk to you." Henry had been quick to his feet and out of the chair that was holding Rachel's coat.

"If it's about Sam—"

"I don't care about Sam."

"Neither does Mum."

She looked between the two of them, Henry's retort said so quickly after Rachel's that it was almost simultaneous. Elizabeth had no idea what was happening. Ten minutes ago, she had been in her study as she and Sam waited each other out, waiting for the other to call time on their relationship. Five minutes ago, she'd been eavesdropping on an intimate conversation between her son and his birth mother. Two minutes ago, she was rehearsing what she would say to them. Now she realised she had been practising for nothing more than a pantomime.

She looked at Henry who was back in the chair, Rachel's pea coat resting on its high back, looking like a cloak across his shoulders. He was getting so big now. He would be tall, like his father, when he finally finished growing. She didn't know how it had happened, but he was so much like Alex.

Henry's hair was thicker, a lighter shade of brown, and his nose more aquiline whereas Alex's had been concaved. His eyes were piercing blue, with flecks of brown permeating their edges. Alex's had been shades of green that changed with his moods, darker when he was angry and yet so light—the colour of summer grass—whenever he was filled with joy.

Perhaps it was simply his mannerisms that had Henry like his father. The way they hold themselves, the way they crumple into chairs, their Keanu Reeves run—their limbs too long for their torsos to keep pace. She wondered how he had acquired all these traits given he had just eight months to learn them.

She thought of the man—the boy?—that had impregnated Rachel, the man she'd been told not to ask after, not to speak about.

Perhaps Henry was his son.

"Kid, could we have a moment?"

Henry put his mug down, finding an old receipt to act as a coaster, and walked silently out—a quick glance to the mother who'd asked him to leave and a slight squeeze of the hand of the mother who had raised him.

Elizabeth sat in the chair opposite Rachel's coat, turning it to face her on the sofa. It squeaked abrasively across the tiles; she would have scolded Henry had he dragged the wood of the chair against the stone of the floor.

"Why don't you call him Henry?" she eventually managed.

"I call my niece the same." Elizabeth watched as a fond smile crossed Rachel's lips.

"How old is she?"

"Four in May. It's all: 'When I start Big School' this and 'In Big School' that at the moment. When we saw her at the weekend, she begged Andy to be allowed to go to school with her, she explained that nursery is simply too boring."

Rachel pulled out her mobile only to quickly discard it on the sofa. "I was going to show you pictures and then I remembered that my phone's still not magically charged itself."

Rachel spoke as if she were the proud parent, as if the girl were her own. Elizabeth ached for Henry, Rachel had been unable to love him but now was singing a sonnet for this pre-schooler.

"Why are you here?"

"After our phone call at the beach, I did some thinking and I was wondering if I could take Henry to meet Judi and Rob. I think it would help him."

"Who?"

"They're my foster parents. My family. My—"

"Real parents." She nodded, understanding suddenly joining them in the kitchen. She looked at the chair Henry had vacated, Rachel's coat hanging limply from its back. "Thank you," she said to it, grateful that Rachel hadn't gone back to Andy as she had originally intended.

"You'll come too, obviously," Rachel's invitation snapped her attention back to her, "you're not going to let a stranger take your son off to Essex for a day regardless of DNA. I just think it would be good for Henry to see that family, identity, isn't forged by some double helix, it's created through time and energy, not just three minutes on my ba—"

"Thank you," Elizabeth rushed in, her hand suddenly in the air, not wanting to hear any more. "You won't talk about the father, but you'll tell me about the conception?"

"You know why I can't talk about the father." Rachel looked at her softly.

"No, I don't."

"All Henry had of me was a name and glimpse at a train station, three days later he's knocking on my door riffling through my mail. At least I knew about the kid, I knew that this could, would, come. Daniel has no idea, it's not fair to him."

"None?"

"I found out I was pregnant in the February half term of Lower Sixth, I didn't return to school after that. I haven't spoken to anyone at school since, because I didn't exactly want to be The Lesbian *and* The Girl That Got Pregnant."

"I was Mo Mowlam," Elizabeth smiled at her wryly, "I had a really bad haircut," she added after a pause, "and a penchant for getting into very heated political discussions in the Sixth Form Common Room."

"Wasn't she bald?"

"Not in 1994."

Suddenly the room was filled with laughter, a laughter that pushed against all four walls and fought against the glass of the windows. Elizabeth tried to find a frame of reference for the sound emanating from the younger woman before her, but found she could compare it to nothing she had ever heard before. It was simply pure, unadulterated joy.

"Do you like curry?" she asked once Rachel's laughter abated.

Rachel

SHE PULLED OUT her keys from her coat and instinctively stuck her foot in the doorway in anticipation of Pete running out into the hall. She nudged him back as she pushed her way through the small gap between door and frame, offering him reassuring noises whilst trying to enter as quietly as possible.

"You don't call, you don't write . . ." Andy's voice rang out from the sofa.

"My phone died."

"And Marc doesn't have an iPhone charger?"

Andy was on her feet, arms filled with the cat, both sets of eyes looking at her accusingly. Hers were framed by her glasses, she had clearly been reading when Rachel had walked in, pyjamas still on. An old pair of Marks and Spencer's bottoms were matched with an ancient University of Sussex rugby shirt Andy had stolen from her years ago. Rachel couldn't remember the name of the girl she, herself, had liberated it from. Rachel had never confessed to Andy that she'd never played rugby, that she didn't even understand the rules.

"I didn't ask." Rachel told a half truth, dropping her keys on the table by the door as she kicked off her trainers. "I'm just going to change—"

"I'll put the kettle on."

". . . and then I'm going to Judi's," she finished as if uninterrupted.

"For how long?"

All Rachel gave her was a shrug, while Pete pushed his head farther into her hand as she stroked him, trying to ignore the awkwardness between herself and Andy. They'd lived in the flat for nearly four years now, and while it had often felt small—especially when Andy had company—it had only once felt as suffocating, and that was when Henry had been standing on the doormat demanding entry.

She squeezed past Andy into her room, hoping for an escape, fresh underwear and a new application of antiperspirant, but she found none as she was followed in first by Andy and then by Pete who jumped, lazily, onto her bed and settled himself beside the bag she'd started to pack, poking his head inside as if to check her supplies. As she moved him away her hand fell on her phone charger. She looked up at Andy.

"You'll charge your phone."

She couldn't tell from the inflection if it was a question or a command. She nodded her reply.

"And you'll answer if I call?"

"Ands—"

"Marc texted me." Andy was sat beside Pete now, one hand moving slowly between his ears. It was the thumbing of the jumper she'd just placed in the bag, almost in a state of carphology, by the other hand that had Rachel suddenly worrying. "Said you're—"

"I'm not." Rachel joined her on the bed, determinedly keeping the cat and bag between them. "Henry's mum, Elizabeth, is, *was*," she corrected, "with Marc's brother. They're fighting and so he was there when I stayed at Marc's. Have we ever met him before?" she asked after a pause.

Andy frowned, hands still busying themselves. "I don't think so. He's mentioned a half-brother, but I didn't think they were close."

"If we'd got to his housewarming at a decent time, we would have met them. Elizabeth and Sam that is."

"This whole thing stinks of serendipity."

"The John Cusack film?" Andy pushed her away, which Rachel took as an excuse to get off the bed. Quickly and unashamedly she changed her clothes for clean ones, finished gathering up her things and threw the bag over her shoulder. As she was about to leave the room, she saw Henry's folder sitting on her bedside table which she folded in half, lengthways, and shoved it in her bag. Another glance to the bed and the girl sitting upon it sent Rachel under it and into a box she'd never unpacked–*Milner 9*–the Tottenham Hotspurs kit joined the rucksack as well.

"If you call, I'll answer," Rachel told her softly before closing the door to her bedroom.

* * *

She hadn't realised how far they'd travelled until Elizabeth changed music from whatever Henry had running through the Aux lead to the radio where eloquent people were discussing perennials. The conversation had tailed off naturally, and she'd found herself looking out of the window at the cars they passed and the passengers they contained. Where Elizabeth had been hard to talk to over a shared meal of almost shepherd's pie, forced niceties and small talk that couldn't fill the room, she was now pleasant company. As if a weight had been lifted from her and she was free to simply be. Rachel was sure, where Elizabeth was so used to Henry's questions, she could simply ask the woman what had changed, but she feared that if she broached the subject Elizabeth would retreat again. Rachel found she didn't want that. She looked across at her, and Elizabeth simply nodded at the boy asleep in the back.

"Any journey longer than thirty minutes." She used the rear-view mirror to smile fondly at her son. "When he had croup, I considered hiring Brands Hatch just to keep us in the car."

"How's he going to cope when he learns to drive?"

"He's fine in the front seat. Last time we drove up to Scotland he bored me rigid, regaling me with the season of The Invincibles. I banished him to the backseat as soon as we hit a service station just so I could get some peace."

"I grew up in Epping, so there's only one North London club."

Elizabeth turned away from the road and looked at her sheepishly. "I have no idea what that means, or how that connects to our conversation."

"No wonder you raised an Arsenal fan." She smiled back at her.

"My father is the most disappointed, he played for Harlequins for a time. He tried so hard to get Henry into rugby too, but Henry was never into sport—like Alex, in that respect—until he came home from school and wouldn't stop."

"How old was he?"

"If you ask him, he will tell you it was his first day of school, but it wasn't until he was seven though and he had James—"

"James?"

"Mr Holt," she corrected quickly.

"James," Rachel repeated, a knowing smile toying with her lips.

"Don't." She was warned, watching as Elizabeth looked into the rear-view mirror at the boy asleep in the back. "Henry doesn't know."

"I think you'll find he knows a lot more than he lets on," she told her, eyes turning to the boats as they crossed the River Medway.

* * *

As the Sat Nav took them through Epping, she watched as Elizabeth's hand darted backwards and instinctively found Henry's knee.

"Time to wake up, Hen," the mother gently coaxed her son, hand returning to the wheel, "we're nearly there."

Henry grumbled softly, head lifting from the window, eyes

opening slowly. "You turned off Morrissey."

"I lived through The Smiths the first-time round, I don't need to again," Elizabeth told him, passing back his phone and cable without so much as a glance. "I'm sure whatever girl—" Rachel instantly spun round in her seat to face him, a smile enveloping her face, ". . . has got you into him will cope without making me suffer too."

"Girl?" she teased him.

"Thanks Mum."

"Girl?" Rachel repeated. "What's her name?"

"There is no girl."

"Caitlin tells me it's Alyssa, one of his friends from school," Elizabeth told her quietly, turning into the cul-de-sac as the Sat Nav had instructed. "Which one?"

"Number Seven. Green door, with . . . shit!" she spotted two cars in the driveway. "My brother's here."

"You didn't call ahead?" Elizabeth scolded as she came to a stop outside the house.

"I didn't call ahead," she nodded. "I guess Henry's impulse control—"

"Or lack thereof."

". . . is inherited." She sighed, letting down her hair, just to quickly tie it back up into a lose bun. "Do you mind waiting here for a sec?"

Without lingering for a response, Rachel got out of the car and headed up the path to her childhood home.

Waiting for someone to open the door, she fiddled with her hair again, it was half plaited by the time the door was opened, a child jumping from Judi's arms to her own.

"El!" Rachel left her hair to be forgotten as small arms wrapped around her neck.

"Hiya, kid," she smiled, holding the child further away so she could see her face and the polyester dress she was wearing. "Who are we today?"

"Elsa."

"Of course." Rachel smiled, plopping her down. "Why don't you go find some toys and continue making a mess of Granny's living room?" She looked up at the woman who'd handed the girl to her. "Hi," she said, before being pulled into a hug.

"How are you doing, my little girl?"

"Thirty-three," Rachel held her close, "I'm thirty-three now."

"You'll always be my little girl," Judi told her, letting her go, eyes hovering a little too long at the faces watching them from the car. "You going to tell me about your girlfriend?"

Rachel ran her fingers back through her hair, undoing the unfinished plait and tying it into a pony tail.

"Not my girlfriend," she said very quickly, almost turning the three words into one. "Have a look at the kid."

Rachel did not need to turn back to know he was staring, practically pressed up against the window.

"Oh my God, he looks just like that O'Reily boy." Judi turned back to look at her. Rachel took her lower lip between her teeth and nodded. "Oh my God."

Judi was off, almost running to the car.

Elizabeth had stepped out, but Henry was not as quick, and his door was pulled open by eager hands. Rachel followed slowly in Judi's wake, stopping by Elizabeth's side, watching as Judi held Henry by his shoulders, having sorted out the collar of his coat, and inspected him.

"Jesus," she breathed, "he's the spitting image of—"

"Yes. I know," Rachel interjected quickly.

"He has your eyes though."

Judi looked back at her, finally releasing Henry from her grasp.

"It's all very *Harry Potter*." Rachel nodded. "Judi, this is Henry. Henry, this is Judi."

He offered her his hand.

"I was the first person to hold you." She ignored his polite gesture and pulled him into a hug.

"Judi. Judith! *Mum!*"

The woman let go of him and looked round, startled at Rachel's outburst.

"This is Elizabeth Cole," Rachel pointed to the woman standing awkwardly beside her, arms folded protectively across her chest. "Henry's mother," she added.

"I'm so sorry." Judi straightened and held out her hand for Elizabeth. "Judi Milner, I'm Rachel's mum."

"I know, she's spoken a lot about you." Rachel watched Judi's eyes change, wording a question without asking it. "Rachel's spoken a little about you," Elizabeth corrected.

Elizabeth's hand was swallowed up by Judi's other. "Rachel's not much of a talker." And Rachel could sense Elizabeth tense as Judi held her hand between hers for too long.

"You going to let us in or do you want us to stay on the pavement, give the neighbours a show?" Rachel asked, nodding inside to where her niece was now being held in place by her sister-in-law.

Drinks were drunk, banal conversation was passed around them with biscuits, and Olivia sat on her lap colouring pictures of Disney princesses while they spoke about anything other than the obvious. The boys were all out fishing. *You know the lake they like. Do you ever fish?* Anna was a much better feminist role model than Elsa, Mulan was better still. *No, El, Aurora wears pink.* Henry was taking maths, history, sociology and film studies A Levels; Rachel had taken English literature, history and politics. *El, you're not colouring right, colour properly.* Imogen was a mental health nurse, Elizabeth was a business analyst, and Rachel still didn't know what was going to happen to the company after the vote. This was how it continued until Olivia asked her where Andy was and if Elizabeth was Rachel's new girlfriend. Imogen smiled apologetically at Elizabeth and swept her daughter up into her arms, talking about putting on a DVD as they hastily departed for any other room.

"She's adorable." Elizabeth smiled round the table's remaining guests. "I can see why you're so taken with her."

"Rach is a lot better with Luke's two than Tom's son."

Rachel looked at her watch. "Fifty-two minutes." She half smiled at the woman opposite. "You managed to go nearly an hour, impressive." She deadpanned as she pushed back her chair and headed to the front door where she'd dropped her bag.

She was upstairs and plugging in her charger, the sad red battery icon joined by the lightning bolt as she turned on the electricity. She held the object between her hands and waited for it to burst to life before her. When she glanced up, she saw Henry looking around her childhood room. Unlike her brothers'—changed and tailored to fit the needs of family visits—hers had been left untouched and still bore all the hallmarks of the student who had spent summers back home. Amnesty International posters, maps of faraway countries she had wanted to visit, photos of friends and nights out. There were a couple too many of Andy.

"Your mum seems nice," Henry ventured as the phone went from black to white, suddenly a hive of activity.

"She is." Rachel nodded.

"What was she talking about?" he asked, sitting beside her.

"Rhys, Tom's son, is twelve."

She started slowly, not really sure how she was going to continue or how far she would take it.

"When he called me, told me that he and his fiancé were having a baby, I didn't take it very well."

The phone was making angry noises, notifying her of messages and voicemails she'd missed. She flipped a switch on the side to put it on silent.

"I got really drunk, one of my friends had to take me to hospital—that kind of *really drunk*. They," she nodded downstairs, "had to come pick me up from Brighton. When I went back, I kept drinking. Don't really remember my last few months at Sussex. Rhys was born the summer you turned four while I managed to graduate with a third and liver damage. Thank God for regeneration," she finished softly, idle thumbs unlocking her mobile and starting to wander through the barrage of messages she'd received in the past eighteen or so hours.

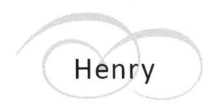

Henry

HENRY HAD HAD several rehearsals as to how it was going to go. He had gone up and down London Road on Google Street View, finding that there were shops on one side and old town houses on the other. He had planned the route from the station, discovering that it would take him thirteen minutes to walk along the road, or fifteen if he took a pedestrian path. Both routes he had memorised using Google Street View. He'd found a Costa in the town centre he could double back to if he got there and nobody was home. He knew the times of all the return trains. He knew that if he got stuck in Ashford his mother would diligently come to pick him up. She would complain and tell him about being a responsible adult, having to make journeys home by himself, but he knew she would come to get him regardless.

Henry had planned for everything. He had three conversations prepared depending on how Rachel King answered the door, a fourth in case Andrea Gregory opened it instead.

However, none of his careful organisation that had him equipped for the moment he spoke to his birth mother had foreseen him sitting on her teenage bed looking up at a map of Cuba with a poster of Che Guevara beside it looking back at him.

"You're somewhat of a cliché," he told her after a while, tired of having Che's eyes boring down at him.

"Says the boy that listens to music to get into girls' pants."

"You ever been to Cuba?"

"No." She shook her head sadly. "Never made it."

"What happened?"

"Andy." Her smile remained doleful, her eyes fixated on her phone.

He pushed himself off her bed and walked around her room, hovered around the various photographs Blu-Tacked to her wall, ran his fingers over her desk and picked up odd knick-knacks she'd gathered over the years: a piece of the Berlin Wall encased in plastic, a small purple stone, a tiny figurine of Buddha, just to put them back down exactly where they'd lain, perfectly placed in their circles of dust, trying to pretend they hadn't been moved at all. It was at the framed picture of a younger Judi holding one of Rachel's nephews that he stopped and turned to face her again.

"Are you happy?" he asked her, the picture still in his hand.

She shrugged, and stood with him at her desk, taking the picture from him and replacing it.

"My dad wasn't happy," he told her, watching as she, too, tried to marry the picture with the pattern of dust that had formed around it.

"Wasn't he?"

He shook his head. "Mum says his death was an accident."

He watched her open and close her mouth. She didn't know. She must have created another reason for his absence. Assumed they'd divorced, like everyone else's parents. Apparently 42% of marriages end in divorce; he remembered reading that from one of his sociology textbooks.

"You looked sad when I saw you in London."

He looked back at the picture of Judi holding one of her grandchildren. She was smiling so broadly at the sleeping baby, his head covered in a blue knitted cap, his hands in mittens to stop him scratching. "I can't be sad too."

Suddenly, he was being held, her cheek pressed tightly against his, her arms strong and warm around him. He didn't realise he was crying until he felt the tendrils of her hair dampen between them.

She held him tighter and hummed softly into his hair, flattening it over and over with her right hand, as her left drawn circles between his shoulder blades with her palm.

He pushed himself away and wiped at his eyes, the word sorry emerging abashedly from his lips as he did so.

"Why do you think you're going to be sad?"

Rachel was leaning against her desk now, hands holding the picture of Judi and the baby again, rather than him.

"You looked sad—"

"You said that."

Her eyes wavered between him and the photograph. "You didn't answer when I asked if you were happy."

"There's a difference between not being happy and being sad."

"I can't be sad."

This wasn't supposed to be how it happened. He was going to knock on her door. They were going to talk. She was going to introduce him to Andrea Gregory, they were going to be cute and married and lesbian together. They were going to be happy. She was going to be happy. She had to be happy. So he could be happy. He had to be happy. He had to be brilliant. Like his father was brilliant.

His timeline was getting longer. It was becoming like Grace's.

Birth.	Birth.
Court case.	Adoption.
Foster home.	Preschool.
Appeal.	Primary School.
Foster home.	Secondary School.
Preschool.	History class.
Failed adoption.	Grace running out of history.
Foster home.	Ignoring Grace in school.
Primary School.	GCSEs.
Foster home.	Sam moving in.

Foster home.	Seeing Rachel at St Pancras.
Secondary School.	Finding Rachel on the internet.
Foster home.	Dover.
History class.	Awkward meal in the kitchen.
Crying.	Mum and Sam fighting.
Running.	Rachel sitting on the sofa.
GCSEs.	Crying in Essex.
Gone.	Being held by Rachel.
Now?	Now?

Rachel wasn't happy though, she was the epitome of broken: in a fucked-up relationship with her best friend, locking herself in bathrooms, running away from conversations with her mother, fiddling with her hair when she's nervous, and unable to cook.

Yet she was holding him again, humming that same song as before, rubbing the same circles between his shoulders as she flattened the same hairs on his head.

"People get sad, it's okay to be sad sometimes."

"What if she gives me up because I'm sad?"

She pushed him roughly away from her, her hands suddenly squeezing at his shoulders rather than trying to soothe him with their palms. "She is not going to give you up."

Her words were angry; he didn't know why she was so angry with him.

"They didn't want a sad one. That's why they chose me. I have to be happy."

"You don't *have* to be anything."

Her back was bowed, she was searching out his eyes, but he wouldn't meet them.

"You gave me up," he said entreatingly.

She cradled his face between her hands and pulled it up, so he had to look at her.

"To a couple that promised to love you. To a couple that told me you would be the most loved little boy in all the world."

"Well that didn't work!" he spat at her as stepped out of her hands.

"What do you want from me, kid?" Just as quickly as he'd been pulled into her arms, she was pacing around small room like a caged animal. "I was seventeen when I got knocked up. You think I could have raised you? You think I could have *loved* you?" Her words were angry and bitter. Her movements erratic yet her words so precise— almost practiced—like she'd been waiting to say them to him since he'd first knocked on her door. "I was sixteen when I fucked him. I was angry because Charlotte was bitching at me about how fucking shit it is to be gay, she'd shoved *The Well of* Fucking *Loneliness* in my hands as she dumped me. Told me to read it and find a happy lesbian and for ten minutes there he was, my best friend, and I thought I could give it ago, because anything had to better than being gay."

He was up against the far wall. His legs had hit the small radiator underneath the window. Suddenly he was crashing down it, the hot metal burning through his jumper. He was uncomfortably warm, but he did not move.

"Fuck!" He watched as she collapsed against the opposite wall, her legs jutting beneath her, as her hands tangled in her hair.

"I thought that by bringing you here," she said eventually, all the anger gone from her voice so only sadness remained. "Getting you to meet Judi and my family, it would answer all your questions, but I don't think I thought about it enough."

"What do you mean?"

"You try so hard to tell yourself that you're whoever you want to be, that you are your own person, but we're not. We're our parents' children. We just happen to have more parents than other people."

He noticed there were glow in the dark stars on her ceiling. He'd had some too; his mum had tried to arrange them into constellations. She'd managed Orion's Belt and The Plough before getting irate and sticking them randomly. He'd taken them all down once he'd touched Alyssa's breast. He didn't think she'd let him do it again if she came into his room and saw it littered with plastic stars. Now he was touching so much more as they listened to The Smiths and The Cure.

"What we have to decide is which parents we want to be like…"

"Nurture or nature."

"Before I lived here, I lived with a couple called Tony and Debbie who had this dog, Sheila. They moved to Spain, taking the dog but leaving me behind. I called them Mum and Dad. Then I had my actual mum and dad. Some days they were spies, travelling to exotic locations on secret missions, for Queen and Country. Other days they were Jor-El and Lara and I was sent to Earth because my planet was dying."

He looked across at her she was looking up at the stars too.

"I had always promised myself that I would never do that to a kid. That that was the worst way to grow up. To have that not knowing constantly hanging over you." Tears were falling freely down her face, and she wasn't bothering to stop them. "It leaves an ache that can't be explained. The *why didn't they want me?* And the *what did I do wrong?* I told you that I grew up not wanting to ask those questions because I didn't want it to be me. I didn't want to know what I had done wrong. I promised myself that I would never allow another human to feel that way." A smile briefly crossed her face. "A promise I thought would be so much easier to keep when I realised just how much I wanted to touch my best friend's boobs and what that meant." She stopped to wipe her eyes, as if only just realising that she was crying.

"But you got pregnant," Henry finished for her.

"But I got pregnant." She nodded.

She turned away from the stars and looked back at him; she patted the space next to her on the carpet and he crawled over to her. Wrapping an arm around him and laying a tender kiss upon his temple, she whispered into his hair, "I'm sorry I broke my promise."

Elizabeth

HENRY WAS STILL upstairs with Rachel when the others returned. The quiet, overly polite conversation between her and Judi was cut off by a cacophony of noise: wellington boots being kicked off at the back step, fishing rods clattering together as they were leant against the outside wall of the kitchen. An eight-year-old snatching a mobile phone from his grandfather and running into the other room to show his mother all the fish he'd caught. Two men sizing her up and down as they dished out the fish and chip supper they'd bought home en route.

She'd been introduced as Rachel's friend. Luke had laughed at his mother, told her it was the twenty-first century, she didn't need to be Rachel's friend. The father, Rob, he'd called himself, as he shook her hand, told her he was glad she wasn't Andy. Elizabeth thought she heard him refer to the absent woman as a whore, her suspicions confirmed when Judi remonstrated him with a sharp *Robert!* as she took a chip from one of the plates.

It was all going as well as could be expected until Luke asked where Rachel was hiding, that it was unlike her to be so far away from food.

"She's upstairs with . . ." Judi had no end to her sentence though. She was looking to her to complete it for her. But Elizabeth didn't know the end to it either.

She simply rose and left the room, passed the stairs and out the front door. She opened up her car and sat in the driving seat. No keys

165

in the engine. Just sat there, her fingers drumming out a nervous rhythm on the steering wheel.

She had always been quiet, even after moving out of her parents' house into the flat in Fife she'd shared with Caitlin she remained quiet—two only children slotting into the stereotype of introverts perfectly. Alex had always been too serious, too reserved to speak much louder than a whisper. He'd always told her that if he had to shout to be heard, likelihood was that he wouldn't be saying anything worth hearing. *Even Scottish independence?* she'd asked. *Especially Scottish independence,* he'd replied.

She had never intended to raise Henry in the same manner, she wanted him to have the confidence to master any situation, to conquer the world. *Turn your fears into possibilities,* was the mantra she'd given him. However, with only herself as a guide, only her example to follow, he too was quiet.

She didn't find fault in that, though a lot of people did. James had suggested football as a means to get him out of his shell, to get him interacting with the other kids in the class, but even with football in his life Henry seemed quite content remaining in his 'shell'. He just didn't seem all that bothered by other people. Much in the same way she had never been overly concerned with others.

Matt had once asked if she had considered testing him for autism. Asperger's had a big thing in Brussels at the time, apparently Henry's idiosyncrasies fit into a lot of what they were discussing on the continent. Elizabeth had decided that even if she did, even if he was, it wouldn't change anything. He was simply Henry. Anyway, she'd met children with autism, they weren't like Henry: they had meltdowns in supermarkets, they bit and spat, they were mute. Henry was simply quiet, like she was quiet, like his father was quiet.

But here she was in a house filled with people, with excited chatter surrounding her, of *the fish was this big,* of *come here let me show you the pictures,* and she suddenly wondered what Henry would have been like if he'd had all this. If he'd had a house filled with people, with excited chatter surrounding him instead of the dulcet tones of James Naughtie and Sarah Montague telling them about the world around them as they ate breakfast in relative silence.

She didn't know how long she'd been sitting, staring forward at a house identical to the one Rachel had grown up in, as they were all identical in the cul-de-sac, when the car sunk lower with the weight of another.

"Your family must think me terribly rude," she told Judi, her eyes not deviating from a cat cleaning its front paws.

"Please, after ten years of Andy you're a breath of fresh air."

She tried to smile at the woman, but it was weak, it sat pathetically on her face.

"I think you're doing remarkably well, given the situation," Judi pressed on, a hand now on hers. It was warm against her skin. It felt like her own mother's on the rare occasions she ever touched her.

"You know, soon Rachel will have been in my life longer than she wasn't. I don't know what I'd do if her birth mother ever came back into her life. She's my little girl. She was at seven, she is at thirty-three, and she will be when she's my age."

She wanted to say something, anything; she opened her mouth, hoping words would follow, but she was quiet. She had always been quiet. There were no words.

So, Judi continued: "I can count on one hand the amount of times she's called me 'Mum' or 'Mummy'. The first was when she thought she might be pregnant. Tears streaming down her face. It wasn't that she didn't know what to do, it's that she was so terrified she'd disappointed me. She called me 'Mummy' and begged me to continue to love her."

Elizabeth looked across at the woman sitting in her car. The severe cut of her short grey hair made her look harder than her words suggested. There couldn't be much of an age difference between Judi and her own mother, yet she could never imagine

167

having this conversation with her own.

"I was so busy preparing for Rachel to tell me she was a lesbian, I must have bought k. d. lang's entire discography and any magazine that featured Ellen Degeneres or Sandi Toksvig. It never occurred to me to warn her about safe sex and contraception. I never thought I'd have to worry about any of that."

"Did you always know?"

"No." She shook her head fondly. "You hear parents tell you that they knew; Rob claims he did, but he didn't. It was Tom that told me. He was living at home while his first divorce was going through, caught her with the Browns' girl." She was pointing across the road at another identical house. "Warned me that I should probably pay closer attention to the sleepovers they had.

"El always seemed so sure of herself, I didn't think that she might have had doubts," Judi finished softly, as if it were her fault her little girl had gotten pregnant, as if it were her fault that Elizabeth was sitting in her car outside her house while her son— Judi's grandson?—was in her little girl's childhood bedroom trying to find himself, forge an identity that he'd felt unable to find with her.

Judi rubbed the back of Elizabeth's hand which was still holding onto the steering wheel. "Come back in when you feel ready. Imogen sent Luke a text while they were out, so they brought back plenty of fish and chips for everyone."

Her hand left hers as Judi went to leave the car. Elizabeth missed the soothing touch of the stranger. "Do you know who she is?"

Her words brought the woman back to her. "I'm sorry?"

"Rachel's birth mother?"

"Oh." Judi sat back down in the passenger seat, her left hand no longer on the handle to leave. "Annabelle King. My social worker—"

"You have a social worker?"

"Rob and I had one until Rachel's nineteenth birthday, Rachel had hers until her twenty-fifth and she left education." She said it as if she'd had to explain it to a lot of people before. "My social worker," she continued, "showed me all of Rachel's paperwork. Her mother wasn't able to look after her, so she wanted to give Rachel up properly. It was only at the behest of her own mother that she was put into foster care rather than adopted. Just in case, you know? She didn't want Annabelle to be unable to change her mind.

"I lived with such a shadow for so long, terrified that each day was going to be the day that Annabelle King came and asked for her child back. That she was ready. That she could be her mother again. That day never came, though."

"Do you think Rachel will . . . ?" she trailed off, worried about the brashness of her question.

"That Rachel will ever look for her?"

Judi shook her head after a nod of her own.

"The reason I can count on one hand the times Rachel has called me 'Mum' or 'Mummy' is because she's had parents, and she's grown up believing they didn't want her. All she wants is to be wanted. She convinced herself, as a child, that if she calls me 'Mum', or if she calls Rob 'Dad', that we might stop wanting her too."

Rachel

SHE HADN'T MEANT to lose her temper. That wasn't how it was supposed to go. She was supposed to give him answers, offer him closure, and he'd leave. She could get on with her life. He could get on with his. And they could put it behind them. Forget it happened and perhaps, in time, it might not have. It would all fade away. She would put it down to a dream and continue. Start again. That's what she was good at. But now she was pulling away from Andy and suddenly finding . . . She didn't know what she was finding, all she knew was that her practiced and well-ordered life had suddenly been thrown into chaos.

She put it down to lack of sleep. She'd spent Friday night on Marc's hideously expensive yet uncomfortable sofa, and Saturday night had been spent in Elizabeth's spare room. She'd wanted to put her restless night down to the draft coming in through the farmhouse's old windows; she knew, however, it was the fact that her room was sandwiched between the child she'd put up for adoption and the woman she'd given him to. The woman who'd been delightful company, who'd stayed up talking with her long after Henry had gone to bed, the woman who was downstairs talking with her mother and sister-in-law.

No, it was lack of sleep. It had to be lack of sleep.

Rachel had told Elizabeth that she'd known this day could—would—come. She should have prepared for it better. Had a speech worked out. Anything was better than a trite explanation about the fact that she was just a child herself when he was conceived.

There was so much she could have done or not done to prevent this moment.

Yet there was a boy, her child, sitting opposite her, his knees wrapped in his arms looking up at the stars stuck to her ceiling.

Judi would have loved him, just as Judi loved her. Judi would have helped raise him as she'd helped raise her. Judi, the only person to hold him before he was passed between social workers and into the arms of Elizabeth Cole in the next room. Judi, who had held him because she herself couldn't, who had instantly fallen in love with him where she hadn't.

Judi would have kept him, would have worshipped him, because he was the child of her own little girl. But because Judi loved her so, she helped her find others who could love him more than she could at seventeen. Judi, because she loved her so, answered the phone and the door, intercepted questions and helped hide her away from the world until she was ready to face it again. Kept her hidden in her room, at her own request, while a child continued to grow inside her and then again as her mind and body recovered from its absence.

Guilt suddenly washed over her. Henry shouldn't be here, he simply shouldn't exist.

She shouldn't have had sex with Daniel all those years ago, she shouldn't have used him like that. She should have told him to use a different condom; she knew he'd been carrying that one around with him since he was fourteen. She should have known condoms expire, she should have gone to the doctors and got the morning after pill. Judi would have gone with her and held her hand as she spoke with the GP. She should have realised that all the nausea and vomiting were symptoms, not just part of her anxiety and stress at her new A Level courses.

It was all too much. All too confusing.

Her life had been meandering along quite happily; she had a routine, safety and consistency. She might not have been over-the-moon happy, but she had been content for the most part. Her job paid the bills and left her a healthy disposable income after that, she had Andy, and she had a cat. Well, Andy had a cat, but Pete slept on Rachel's bed more often than not and she fed him each morning.

She looked around the room, to the boy that shouldn't exist, and realised that it was the thought of never seeing a cat again that lingered most on her mind. Her eyes caught on the map of Cuba, the poster of Che Guevara, suddenly to the countless photos from countless nights out. Her brothers' rooms had changed, why hadn't hers? Why hadn't she changed from the girl she was at university?

She was thirty-three. It was time she moved on.

"Sorry." The word was quiet, barely a whisper, but she knew he'd heard it.

"For what?"

"I think . . ." She pulled her legs up so she too was hugging her knees, her cheek resting upon them, the sharpness of the bone keeping her focused. "I think a lot of that was aimed at my mother."

"Judi?"

"My other one."

"Do you wish you were normal? Like with just one set of parents normal, not like straight no—"

"I get it, kid, stop digging your hole." She smiled weakly at him. "And all the goddamned time. I'm thirty-three and I miss them, you know?" He nodded. "How can I miss someone I've never met?" Her soliloquy was broken by a scoff. "I'm sorry that you had to go through that too. I was angry and hurting and just wanted ten minutes to be like everyone else. We used protection—"

"I—"

"Yeah, that's too much isn't it?" She looked across at him, eyes just like her own shining back at her.

He looked up to the stars again before shifting his weight and crawling across the room to her.

"I'm sorry, kid." She wrapped an arm around him as she held

him close for the fourth time in an hour, for the fourth time in his life. "I can't tell you about him."

"I don't think I want to know." He rested his head on her shoulder. "I already have a father I don't know that I get compared to. I don't want another."

Rachel suddenly understood: it wasn't her he was searching out. He wanted to know about his dad, about Elizabeth's late husband, she was just collateral amongst all the questions he couldn't ask his mother.

That feeling, that sudden need to flee the farmhouse on Friday evening returned. The boy had come, he'd asked his questions, and he would surely leave.

The night before would mean nothing. The takeaway they'd shared, dipping naan bread into the various curries they'd ordered, the greasy drips on the coffee table as a movie carefully selected, and then woefully ignored, playing on the television as they talked. Arsenal had lost to Chelsea in the late kick off, Tottenham had won their earlier game. Spurs were ahead in the league by a couple of points.

Not for long, Henry had tried to convince them as Elizabeth rolled her eyes at the pair of them from the sofa.

Yesterday was just playing make believe. Playing house in someone else's life.

"You should tell your mum."

"Tell her what?

"That you're sad."

"I'm not sad."

"Then why did you stalk me on the internet?"

The question was left to hang in the air between them. The boy who asked nothing but questions was now unable to answer. He made no buzzer sound, no hand signal, just left the question between them, adding it to a growing list of unanswered ones in his life.

"All right then." She smacked her thighs as she prepared to stand; the sooner she ended this conversation, the sooner he would leave. And he would leave. As the other members of her family—families—had left before him. There was no sense in prolonging it. "You hear that racket coming from downstairs?"

Henry sat up with her and nodded.

"The men have hunted and gathered for us."

He frowned at her but stood up nonetheless.

"Don't look so worried, they went to the fish and chip shop."

"We don't eat cod."

It was her turn to look confused.

"Overfishing."

Rachel had no response to that, so she headed to the door and reached for the handle, her hand was around its cold brass before he called her back.

"El?" he tried tentatively.

The name felt wrong coming from his mouth, it had come from Rhys, who had struggled with the first syllable as a toddler and only been able really to enunciate the second. Slowly the rest of them had started to call her that too. She wasn't sure that Olivia even knew that her name was Rachel, she was simply Auntie El to her. That was what her family called her, that was their name for her. Andy had tried it once and she'd quickly put a stop to it: only Milners got to call her by that particular moniker.

But Henry was family too, wasn't he? She'd carried him for nine months and given birth to him. They shared DNA, and he had her eyes. Blue, flecks of brown. Did he not get to call her that too?

"Your phone is ringing," he told her, delivering her the vibrating mobile.

She looked at the caller's name displayed on the screen. A goofy photo of Andy shined up at her. She was in a wig and wearing too much make up, dressed as Felicia when Marc had taken them to see *Priscilla Queen of the Desert*. Marc had given Andy a lecture about misappropriating Drag Culture, but Andy had just blown a kiss at him and told him he was jealous because she made a prettier Queen than he did. Marc had looked to Rachel for help, but when it came to Andrea Grigoriadis, she was helpless.

Rachel let the phone ring and sent Andy to voicemail. She placed her down beside the framed photograph of Judi holding baby Henry—or was he baby King? The way Judi looked down at him—with such love and affection—perhaps he was a baby Milner. Maybe, in another life, he would have been a Spurs fan, bored them all with tales of Lineker and Gascoigne, of King and *my club my one and only club*, of Kane and *he's one of our own,* singing songs of Ali only costing five mil, being better than Özil. He would have gone fishing at the weekends and had a slight, ever so slight, Estuary accent like the rest of the Milners.

"It's too late for the cod. They're battered and plated by now. Might as well eat them," she told him, pulling open the door and praying he would once again follow her.

His eyes flicked back to the photograph of Judi on the desk. The picture of Judi holding him looking down at him with such adoration, like he was the most precious thing in all the world simply because he was hers, he was her own little girl's. That's why she kept the photograph on display, not because she wanted to keep the memory of the baby she gave away, but because of the look in Judi's eyes, the love written across her features. She kept the picture to remind her that she would always be loved by the woman who had raised her. She would continue to be loved regardless.

"What did you want to be when you grew up?" he eventually asked.

"A political journalist," she told him, her clammy hand dropping from the door knob as they were clearly no closer to returning downstairs. "I had these grand visions of sitting on a balcony in Paris, a typewriter on a table, the Eiffel tower in the background, a cigarette perpetually balancing between my fingers."

"So, you wanted to be a journalist during the Second World War?"

"You've got a quick wit for someone so unsure of himself," she told him, hands in her pockets rubbing the sweat away on the fabric inside.

He simply shrugged, eyes never wavering from the photograph surrounded by dust.

"What do you want to be?"

Another shrug in lieu of a response.

"You've got the world ahead of you. You can be whatever you want to be."

"Mum says I'm going to be brilliant. My dad was brilliant."

"You could be a beggar or a bum, and she'll still love you."

He tore his eyes from the photograph on her desk. "How do you know?"

"Because mine loves me regardless. Yours will too."

Henry

HIS MUM HAD suggested they go to his grandparents for the rest of the week, trying to bribe him with a camping trip with his grandfather, as she was typing in various addresses into her Sat Nav trying find the quickest route home, theirs or her parents', from Essex. Henry had attempted to laugh the idea away—told her that one of his mothers needed to be responsible, that they couldn't both go running to their parents when life got weird. The endeavour fell flat, so he tried a different tact. He'd insisted that they go back to Kent, told her that he wanted to clear his head and take Thatcher for a walk in the woods. She had suggested that she might come too, but he had told her that she needed to go back to work, it didn't matter how senior she was—she had to go back eventually. She had made him call Caitlin within her earshot, to make the arrangements in front of her so she could make sure he was going where he said he was and not on another impromptu trip to his birth mother.

Caitlin had picked him up from Sevenoaks station after lunch on Monday; she closed the cattery in the afternoons so she could tend to her own animals. Henry now sat on the edge of a bench, watching Caitlin brush one of the horses. He didn't know which one it was, he could never tell the brown ones apart. He knew the grey one was called Solo, but the brown ones were interchangeable. He called them both Twix, it seemed simpler that way; besides, they were horses, they didn't know they had names.

He was picking at a piece of the splintering wood when he finally ventured. "Why didn't you adopt? Like, you and Matt have been together forever, you're practically married. Didn't you two ever want kids?"

He looked up when he no longer heard the sound of the brush meeting the hair. The woman stood frozen in place, the horse continuing to chew on an errant bit of straw.

As the silence between them grew longer, Henry braced himself for a buzzer sound to come from his godmother's mouth, but instead, "I've been pregnant three times that I know of—"

"Wha—"

"Henry," Caitlin sighed, clearly already exhausted by the conversation that had barely begun, "this is difficult for me, I can either tell you or you can ask questions, I can't handle both."

She looked down at him briefly enough to catch his nod of acquiescence before turning back to the horse and resuming her ritualistic brushing.

"Rose survived the longest. From the first night I discovered I was pregnant I started reading to her. By twelve weeks, Matt started too. Stroked my growing stomach and read aloud from whatever book was on the go at the time. At twenty weeks, we found out she was a girl, so your mum went through books of baby names with me and found the name Rose. Apparently its Germanic, it can mean fame or it can mean kind."

He looked up at her as she paused and saw her shrug her shoulders.

He didn't know what he should do, he suddenly didn't feel as though he wanted to know, that it was all too much. He knew in these sorts of situations people hugged, but he didn't know if that was acceptable. Would she want to be comforted by someone like him? Surely she'd want to be held by Matt or his mother. An equal. Not by a seventeen-year-old. He didn't think he would be able to fix the sadness that he'd caused her to remember, to bring to the surface. So, he just sat rigidly on the cold wood of the bench, the splinters he was picking at catching under his nail, the pain adding to his discomfort as his Godmother bared her soul, her own pain, before him.

"It was during her twenty-fifth week that she stopped moving."

Caitlin had stopped brushing the horse, but the instrument was still pressed against one of the Twix's hairs.

"I had carried her for 173 days without an issue, but then my body did what it had done all the times before. The hospital said it was a placental abruption. September 25th 2004 at 5:07 in the afternoon, I delivered Rose and held her in my arms. I would have held her forever had Matt not forced me to hand her back to the nurses."

Caitlin was crying now.

He wished so much that she had made a buzzer sound, that she had told him his question was inappropriate, that he should have moved on. He didn't know what to do now she was crying, so he rolled a small splinter of wood between his index finger and thumb as he forced himself to make eye contact with her. He knew he should be stood, he should be hugging her, that's what people did in these situations, yet he found he couldn't move, the weight of her words, of her tears, keeping him on the bench.

"I don't believe in God, or a higher power. I believe in science and evolution and evidence. None of those things think I should have children. That, my dear Henry, is why we didn't adopt like your parents. I'm not meant to be a mother."

"But—"

She raised her hand to stop him. "Matt was tired of the IVF."

"But—"

"We'd just crossed the Millennium, Hen, we had Tony Blair and Girls Aloud, we were still mourning the death of Dianna, the world was a different place."

"Dial-up internet?"

"Dial-up internet," she agreed, giving a final pat to the horse's neck before abandoning any pretence of grooming.

She dropped Twix's brush back in its bucket and threw his stable rug back over him. Her hand ran down the horse's nose before she closed the bottom half of the stable door behind her and left him. He stuck his head out over the door while she whispered something about his laminitis and being able to re-join the others soon, and then there was another touch to his face before she double-checked the latch.

"You answered my questions," Henry breathed as Caitlin sat beside him, hugging the bucket to her chest.

She shrugged. "You seem to be searching for answers."

"I didn't mean to make you cry though."

"It's not your fault my body is a barren wasteland."

Henry didn't know what the reply to a sentence like that should be, so he watched as Caitlin tidied away the equipment, sitting the bucket beside the other two, black joining white and red on the shelf. They remained in silence as she led him out of the stables, a silence he knew couldn't remain, he had to say something, to be able explain why he had asked her the question that had led to her tears. However, the more his brain told him that he had to say something, the less he wanted to say anything at all.

"Mum says they adopted because Dad was sad," Henry managed as he followed her back to the car.

Caitlin looked across the roof at him quizzically before settling into the driver's seat.

The gate was closed behind them and the stables shrunk in the rear-view mirror before she responded.

"What are you talking about?"

"Mum said they didn't have a baby of their own because Dad was sad," he tried again. "They worried that their baby would be sad too."

"Sad seems a pretty weak euphemism for depression, even by your mother's Anglican standards."

Caitlin often referred to his mother as *Anglican*, a catch-all term to try and qualify all of her idiocrasies. His mother didn't go to church though. Caitlin said that she'd not stepped inside one since the death of his father. Henry didn't think that *Anglican* was quite the right word to explain his mother's repression, her inability to discuss anything directly that might disappoint her own conservative mother, despite having moved away from home over twenty years ago.

"I mean—" Caitlin continued talking, seemingly unaware that Henry's focus was far from her. ". . . the man gets rat arsed at two in the morning and ploughs his car into a tree. That's not *sad*. Especially given the first two attempts."

His hands were banging on the dashboard, then they were fumbling with his seat belt, suddenly they were grappling with the door handle trying to pry it open. But the car was too modern, it automatically locked while the car was moving. He needed to get out. The car was screaming at them because his seatbelt was undone, the car knew there was a body on the passenger seat, that the body should have a seatbelt on for its safety. He just needed to get out of the car, to escape the seatbelt which was keeping him trapped.

As soon as Caitlin found a patch of road wide enough for her to pull over without disturbing others, when the car was stationary, he bolted. He threw up in the hedgerow, his pile of vomit illuminated by the flashing of Caitlin's hazard lights, as if everything he had tried to contain within him all these years suddenly needed to be released. All his fears, all his doubts, all his unasked questions manifested themselves as this horrible mess of half-digested sandwich and gastric acid.

Growing up he had always had his father with him. The man he never knew, the man that only existed in photographs and other people's memories, was constantly with him. Henry first noticed him when he was doing something silly in the living room; he was watching TV, there was music playing, and he was miming along with the lyrics as he danced along to the beat. His mum smiled up at him from the sofa and told him how much like his father he was, how his father would sing along to the radio and dance when he thought no one was looking.

Then his father was there when he'd complained about Gordon Brown calling someone a bigot. He didn't understand what Gordon Brown had done wrong; the woman had said something stupid and Gordon Brown had been in his car, so it was not like he meant for her to hear him. Anyway, the woman was wrong and she had been a bigot. His mum had smiled at him, wrapped an arm around him and pulled him close to her. *You're so like your father,* she'd whispered into his hair before kissing his temple.

Soon Henry realised his father was always there, this man that he didn't know but was somehow just like him. All the times Henry thought he was being himself, he was being his father. At first he thought it was a good thing, to be like this brilliant man, to be like the man his mother continued to worship posthumously, but as he grew he found it hard to stand tall when he was forever looking over his shoulder to make sure he was just as brilliant as the invisible man in the room who perpetually followed him around.

The only time his father wasn't with him was when he was playing football, but he often suspected that if his father had liked sport, if his father had preferred to run instead of read, his father would be on the football pitch with him too.

It was Caitlin sat beside him now, though, the seat of her trousers dampening on the cold soil like his. She rubbed circles on his back while he cried as Rachel had done the day before.

"Your mum tells you everything, so I assumed she'd told you that."

"She would have eventually," he acknowledged, "same way she'll talk about you and Mr Holt one day."

As he stared down at the mess from his stomach seeping into

the hedgerow and escaping him further, he wished so much he had just agreed to go to Surrey.

He should have gone camping with his grandfather, they would have built a fire and drank ales from micro-breweries in the local area. Henry would tell him what he thought of each one as his grandfather made notes in his book. They would play chess on the set he'd helped him whittle; his grandfather would beat him but tell him that one day he would lose and on that day, Henry would get to take the set back to Kent. When it got too dark, or too cold, or Henry got too tipsy from the ale, they would retreat into the tent but keep the door open. They would fall asleep, with their heads by the flapping zips, halfway through the stories behind the constellations above them.

The next morning, they would cook breakfast on the fire, they would eat sausages and bacon and black pudding and anything else that had once been a pig, before packing up and returning to 'the women we love'.

That's how his grandfather always referred to his mother and grandmother, 'the women that we love', as if that were their collective noun. Individually they were 'your mother' and 'your grandmother', and sometimes they were 'Elizabeth' and 'Dorothy', and on rare occasions they were 'Betty' and 'Dolly', but whenever he spoke about them together, they were always 'the women that we love'.

His pile of sick had all but disappeared into the grass, making mud where before it had just been dirt.

He wondered what his father had called his mother. If he would have called her Elizabeth or Betty. He wondered if she had been given a pet name or if he gave her his own derivative of Elizabeth; maybe she was Lizzie or Beth. His mum always cried when *Little Women* was on the telly, maybe that's why—it reminded her of his father, the only person that had ever called her Beth.

From what he'd been told, his father had been a staid Scotsman, so perhaps she was always Elizabeth. She would call him Alex, but she would remain Elizabeth to him.

He shrugged away Caitlin's hand and walked back to the car. He sat in the passenger seat, buckled his seatbelt and waited for her to drive him away from the hedgerow.

Elizabeth

A LITTLE AFTER three pm, during the afternoon lull, between the last cup of coffee and the shutting down of the computer, she'd received a text message: *My new number in case you or Henry want to reach me. Rach.*

It was closed with a couple of emojis. She didn't understand emojis, these modern-day hieroglyphics, any more than she understood what was going on in her life. She would show it to Henry, maybe he would be able to explain why she'd been sent a picture of an umbrella followed by a unicorn.

She pulled into her driveway and parked besides Caitlin's Mini, its colour the only similarity to that of the one she'd owned when they lived in Scotland together. She looked over its roof at Sam's grubby Land Rover; she should have told him that she hadn't gone Surrey, that Henry had wanted to remain in Kent.

But it was, technically, his house too. He had given up his home in Ashford for hers in Wye. People were living there now, he'd found tenants remarkably quickly and, apparently, they'd signed a twelve-month contract. He had given up his home and yet she hadn't noticed. He had put faith in her, tried to keep their relationship moving forward when she had been willing to let it stagnate. Maybe it was him that hadn't noticed.

Sam was coming out of the front door as she was locking her car, he must have heard her approach and reasoned it was time for him to leave.

"I needed more clothes."

He smiled sadly at her, rearranging the overnight bag in his hand as their paths crossed. "Thought I would pop by on my way home from work. If I had known you hadn't gone to your parents', I would have got Marcus to show me how to use the washing machine."

"No, no," she waved away his anxious apology, "you need your things. If there is anything I can do to help?"

She glanced down at the brown bag, no bigger than hand luggage, no more than an overnight bag. He was stalling, moving his things little by little, hoping she would change her mind. Hoping she would invite him back.

Sam dismissed her though. He was at the door to his car and she was at the door to her house, her home, before he spoke. "Your friend hasn't returned."

"Rachel's in Essex now," she responded simply, knowing exactly who he was referring to, "back with her parents."

"How do you know?"

"I drove her."

He clucked his tongue, tutting away his annoyance, suppressing the argument he was readying to have with her, clearly considering his words before he accused her of infidelity again.

"You're not the first," he eventually managed.

"I'm sorry?" She turned back to him.

"Straight woman she's done this with," he tried to clarify, but his words made no sense to her. "She's been toying with a girl for years now. Only interested in her when she's in a relationship. Marcus told me all about her. Got this poor girl to break off her engagement for her, only to end their affair as soon as the ring was returned."

There it was. An opening. The chance.

She could let it all out. She could scream and shout. She could lecture. She could theorise. She could explain. All the years, she kept it pent up, locked away, done the right thing. To be the person her mother wanted her to be. The person she was raised to be. *Make the correct choices*, she'd been told. *Your life will never be easy if you make this one, and that's all any mother wants for their child, for them to have an easy life. To have a better life than they had.* It was a choice after all, and she had made hers; Caitlin did not come over to the house anymore.

Soon she found Alex, a man that she loved and adored, who she loved with all of her heart, a man who's grave contained her soul as well as his bones.

She had tried to find others, but it seemed it was Alex or it was no one. Alex was, and always be, the only man for her.

This was her chance to tell him all of that. To explain to Sam why things had gone the way they had. But instead all she could manage was, "Sam." She took his cheek into her hand, the same way she often took Henry's. "One day I might tell you what's going on, but the fact that I won't now should tell you that you should be packing more than an overnight bag. I can tell you this, however." She let his cheek go and straightened his jacket. "I don't know what Marcus has told you, I don't know what you've assumed, but I'm not sleeping with Rachel."

He stilled her busy hands, his attempts to climb into his car abandoned with his overnight bag. He was looking at her like she was the victim in all of this. As if she just had to say the word and all would be forgiven, he would come back, and all this would be forgotten. Rachel King would never have happened.

Just as suddenly, his hand was back at his side and he was bending to retrieve his bag. "Caitlin is in your kitchen drinking your gin."

She closed her eyes, they both knew what that meant.

"When you're ready you'll tell me what's going on, what's wrong?"

"When I'm ready," she nodded.

"You will be ready, won't you?" he asked slowly, suddenly hesitant, desperate not to be rejected again.

That had been her opening, but she let the door close firmly between them.

"Probably not."

She fished out her keys from her bag to avoid the look of disappointment she knew would be etched across his face. When she looked up again, he'd dug his own keys from his pocket and they both made moves to retreat behind their retrospective doors. No goodbyes would be exchanged. No more would be said.

As she heard the thick diesel engine pull away, she silently counted to ten. She hoped the feeling that she was deceiving him would die away once she got to the end. But it remained, weighing heavily in her stomach. She reasoned that she couldn't tell him until Rachel told Marcus—if Rachel told Marcus—it was no longer just her secret to tell. Henry was no longer hers alone.

She slipped out of her heels, shrugged off her coat and hung it besides Caitlin's. She looked around for her slippers before going to find Caitlin in the kitchen. She glanced at the glass in front of her friend, sat neatly between the bottle of gin and a bottle of lemonade. She'd clearly forgotten to restock her tonic from the last time Caitlin had stayed over.

"How many have you had?"

"This will be my third," Caitlin told her as she started to poor another.

"You've called Astrid to get her to look after the cattery or do you want me to do it?"

"I asked her before I drove Henry back."

"And he's all right?"

She nodded. "In his room."

Elizabeth listened for signs of life emanating from the second floor but couldn't find any. "It's very quiet up there, all go okay today?"

She watched as Caitlin downed her drink and pushed away the tumbler.

"Stupid question." Elizabeth sighed, reaching out for her friend's arm. "Come on, help me change the sheets and you can tell me what's wrong."

Caitlin rose from her chair and frowned at her.

"Rachel stayed over Saturday night and I haven't had a chance to change the sheets," she explained as she led her upstairs.

"That's it? You're just going to accept that we're going to argue and that I'm staying over? You don't even want to know what our fight will be about?"

Elizabeth turned to face her on the stairs below. "Either way the result will be the same." She smiled down at her. "What was it you said the other day? Our friendship is older than your teeth? Besides," she turned back and continued on to the guest bedroom with Caitlin in tow, "it can't be any worse than when you arrived drunkenly at my flat and told me that you were sleeping with my lecturer."

"I could be sleeping with your boss," Caitlin mused, slumping down in the armchair in the corner.

"We know damn well you're too devoted to Matt to have an affair." Elizabeth threw across the pillows for her to strip as she started on the duvet. "Come on, out with it."

She tried smiling across at the woman, but Caitlin was having none of it.

"I know you're only drinking so I can't ask you to drive home, you've already booked your place in my spare room and you'll tell me eventually. Or," she went to the wardrobe and pulled out the clean sheets, "do you require more of my gin?"

"You're not going to like it."

"I gathered as much, otherwise you wouldn't have drunk yourself over the limit." Elizabeth sat on the arm of the chair and leaned into Caitlin's shoulder.

"Henry was asking questions," Caitlin fiddled with hem of the bare pillow on her lap, pulling at a loose piece of cotton holding the stuffing in place. "He asked me why Matt and I don't have children, why we didn't adopt."

"What did you tell him?" she asked her softly, leaning in closer so they were practically sharing the chair.

"About Rose," Caitlin said delicately, as if just saying her name caused a fresh tear in a heart. She allowed Elizabeth to pull her close to her, allowed her to kiss her temple and hold her tight. She allowed herself to be comforted. "He then started to talk about why he was adopted. He was telling me about Alex being sad."

She leaned in closer to the warmth of Elizabeth's chest, feeling her tense next to her, as if she feared her next confession would see her banished to the cold.

"I didn't understand. I didn't know what he was talking about."

"You told him."

Elizabeth continued to hold her, unable to do anything else.

"I told him. I didn't know he didn't know. He asks so many questions, I assumed he'd asked that."

Elizabeth was standing now. Her right hand pulling at the fingers of her left, pulling her ring finger back to the point of breaking, her finger and thumb toying with the two rings Alex had bought her.

"Over the years I've honed the art of vagueness." She started pacing. "This is his grandmother's fault." She sighed eventually, dropping down onto the freshly made bed.

"Mother Powell?"

"No, Alex's mother."

Elizabeth sat so her back was rigid, matching the hairs on the back of her neck. Caitlin was still slumped in the armchair, still absentmindedly playing with the loose piece of cotton. "She cornered me at the wake, begged me not to let Henry grow up thinking his father was . . ."

"Was what? Weak? Less than a man?"

Caitlin had sat upright now, mirroring Elizabeth's position on the bed, the pillows piled beside her on the floor as she reached forward for her hands. While it was obvious she was trying to be supportive, the look on her face was incredulous.

"Look, I know that's not the case and you know this, but this was the turn of the millennium. People didn't have mental health issues. People were allowed PTSD or post-natal depression. People did not get to have depression. Men certainly didn't."

"You know suicide is the biggest kil—"

"Don't you *dare* give me the statistics!"

"Fine!" Caitlin flung her arms in the air. "Alex was sad, and when my dad was dying of prostate cancer, he was poorly."

Her life had always been very quiet, Elizabeth found comfort in it. The business of the world around her silenced, the demands and needs of other people gone, and in the quiet there was just her and she could breathe.

Alex had always helped her to breathe. Knowing he was there, that she wasn't alone, that there was someone else that understood, that found the world so confining, unable to meet its demands. Yet he hadn't been able to help her breath for over fifteen years now. She had to remember to do it herself.

In the silence she would count. Count her breaths. Count the days she'd had Henry in her life. Count the days Alex had been gone.

"I thought having Henry, having a child, something to love, something to focus on . . ." Her voice was quiet, her words had been rehearsed for this moment. It was Caitlin that heard them first. She wasn't sure if she'd be able to hold them together if Henry had every asked a question, *the* question, that she would be forced to answer directly. "I thought Henry would be enough. That having Henry would keep Alex with me, give him something to focus on other than his unhappiness."

Tears were falling. Caitlin's hands were wrapped around her own. Her thumb pinned beneath Caitlin's warm skin, Caitlin purposefully holding it tight, so Elizabeth wouldn't be able to rub it raw.

"I was wrong."

Caitlin was trying to sooth her, having pulled her close and whispered loving sentiments in her ear.

"Henry was too much for him," Elizabeth whispered back. "Henry pushed him over the edge."

Rachel

RACHEL WOKE UP softly to the tell-tale signs of her mother in her room. The desperate attempt to quietly open and close the door, the scent of coffee following her in, the sounds of Judi scrambling to find a coaster before setting down the cup. By the time the bed moved with the added weight of her visitor, Rachel was awake.

"I don't want to go to school today," she tried, pulling the sheets tighter around herself.

"Cute," was Judi's response as she gently tugged them back down.

Rachel scrunched her eyes, hoping to force some life into them, before rolling over to the bedside unit. She looked at the clock, sent a distasteful look to Judi, before sitting up and grabbing her coffee.

"I've had like no sleep this past week, why am I awake before twelve?"

"Andy's downstairs."

The hairs prickled on the back of her neck and the smell of the coffee in her hand only added to the sudden wave of nausea.

"Don't look at me like that, if you wanted to hide from your girlfriend, your childhood home was probably not the best place. Now," Judi patted her knee through the covers, "get dressed and come down."

Rachel bit her lip and then tried to form a protest.

"Rachel Milly King, you can either get dressed and face her like an adult, or I'll send Andy up here to you. You've had sex with her enough times in this room, I'm sure she can find her way."

"Yesterday I was your little girl, today you're talking about my sex life?"

"Given that she's no doubt here to talk about Henry, I think it's apt." One last pat on the knee and Judi was standing, and she was at the door when Rachel spoke again.

"Milly?"

"My mother's name was Camilla, had we been allowed to adopt you, that would have been your middle name."

And then the door was shut behind her and Judi's footsteps were heard descending the stairs.

Rachel tried to drink the coffee still in her hands, but it was too hot; there were no delaying tactics to be found within her cup. She threw off the duvet and put on the clothes she found pooled by the foot of her bed. Quickly tying her hair with a band from her wrist, she tried her coffee once more, unsurprised, yet irritated all the same, that it was still too hot to drink.

She grabbed her wallet and phone from the desk by her door and headed out of her room, zipping up her hoody as she closed the door behind her. At the foot of the stairs she found her trainers, squashed her feet into them before trying to rearrange the backs of them so they were comfortable without bending down.

She peered her head around the doorframe of the living room and found Andy flicking through one of Rob's angling magazines, feet tucked under her on the sofa as if the house were her own.

"Come on," Rachel got her attention, "let's go find something to eat, unless you want to keep hearing Judi shush Rob so she can better listen in on us."

"I ate on the train."

"Good," Rachel tried to smile, "means I can have meat without you complaining I'm putting you off your meal." She stuck her tongue out to try and show she was joking, but it all felt very false. The plastic smile Andy plastered on by way of response let Rachel know she'd failed.

* * *

They had exhausted small talk while Rachel walked them up and down the small high street, determined to find somewhere that would suit their need to talk in peace and her appetite. She wasn't sure she was hungry, but a plate of *something* between them was a barrier Rachel felt she needed.

She'd ruled out a café, deciding that alcohol would definitely be needed, but couldn't find a place that was quiet *and* serve her a burger. Apparently the two were binary. Rachel eventually pulled Andy into a small pub down one of the side streets, depositing her at a table in her corner before heading to the bar to get them both drinks.

"Are you moving out?" Andy asked once she'd been handed a glass of red wine and Rachel had slumped herself down in a seat opposite.

"Yes." She looked sadly towards the packet of pork scratchings before her, they were definitely not what she wanted to eat but it was pretty much all the sad little pub had to offer her. She took a long sip from her larger instead.

Andy nodded as she thumbed the rim of her glass. "I don't want you to."

"I need to."

"But why now?"

"Because," Rachel found that starting her sentence was so much easier that finding an end to it. She tugged at her sleeves so they were covering most of her hands and cupped the lukewarm glass in front of her. She definitely should have chosen the Wetherspoons she'd walked passed and deemed too crowded.

"Look," Andy reached out and took her hand, a thing she seldom did in public, "I'm sorry I'm making you do this to my face, but you

197

said you'd answer the phone if I rang and you didn't."

"So, hopping on the train to Essex was your next plan?"

"I was trying to stop you from ghosting out on me."

"I don't ghost," Rachel said quickly before she'd really considered her answer. "What's ghosting?" she asked, sitting back in her chair.

"That thing you do whenever you go on a bad date or when a girl starts to bore you or when Simon from your office wouldn't stop pestering you about joining his five aside team. You stop replying to messages and answering phone calls. In extreme cases you've blocked numbers and left jobs. You disappear on people."

"Oh. Okay, maybe I do that," she conceded.

"Which is why, when you left yesterday, I had you promise to answer my calls."

"And I didn't."

"So here I am." Andy folded her arms across her chest, clearly bracing herself for an argument. "If you're going to break up with me you can do it like a grown up."

"If I'm going to break up with you, we'd have to be in a relationship to begin with."

"Aren't we?"

Rachel had opened her mouth to continue, but Andy's statement stopped her.

"You're not the only one that's had time to think," she told her gently. "And I've had more than I'd anticipated as you've not been answering my calls."

Rachel pushed the remnants of her pint away. She was suddenly in no mood to be drinking. Any Dutch courage she thought she could muster she found she no longer wanted.

"So," Andy continued, "I imagine you would like to discuss monogamy and official titles—"

"Ands—"

"While my sisters will all be fine with it, hell, Callie will want to throw an entire party devoted to the theme of 'I told you so,' my father—"

"Ands!"

Andy pulled her own glass closer towards her. "Don't do this Rach," she said softly to the untouched glass of red wine before her.

Rachel leant across the wobbling table and took the girl's hand; it was warm and clammy where usually her hands were cool. She felt the familiarity of Andy's fingers between hers; the rise and fall of her grandmother's wedding ring on her middle finger; even the lines of ink Andy had tattooed to the side of her palm, linking her little finger to her wrist, were standing to attention.

"We owe each other more than simply being each other's safety nets."

And like that Andy's hand was gone. Snatched away and hidden back beneath the table.

"We love each other." The softness of Andy's tone had been replaced with something more. The words were said almost like a threat, daring Rachel to defy her, to remind her of her place. Ever the devoted lesbian best friend left waiting in the wings. A sad trope in someone else's story.

"I know I'm not easy, I get distracted quickly, and my imagination often leads me down paths I probably shouldn't follow . . ." She trailed off as her hands started to talk for her. Rachel watched them gesticulating wildly to create words Andy couldn't quite articulate.

She took them into her own and stilled Andy's words. Tried to quieten her mind by holding onto her hands.

"The problem is I've always followed you when I should have let you go off on your own."

"But I thought you liked that." Andy's thumb had escaped Rachel's grasp and now rubbing circles on the patch of skin below Rachel's forefinger. "If I remember correctly, I wasn't the only one who hooked up in Budapest."

"But you were the only one to bring someone home and receive a family heirloom as a proposal." Rachel tried to escape Andy's touch but found it forcefully holding on to her, binding her to the conversation.

"This is our life," Andy's smile was as forceful as her hold on Rachel's hand, "we work, gather enough money to take us somewhere, and then burn it, then work until we can do it all again. We're not meant to be like our parents, there's too much to see and do to stay in one place."

"No," Rachel was quick, met force with force and found her hand was released, "this is *your* life. I'm not in my twenties anymore, I can't keep chasing you around hoping you'll stop one day and see me standing there."

"I always see you, Rachel King."

She hated how Andy would say her name and her body would react; Rachel the damned dog to Andy's Pavlov.

"I need for you to more than see me; I need to be enough."

"Can anything be enough in a world this big? Why confine ourselves and try to be small?"

"I don't see settling down as confining or small—"

"I'm not ready." Andy's head was shaking.

"And I think that's why I should move out. Away."

Rachel looked around the dark pub for people listening in. She saw a couple of retired men slouched over the bar, another reading one of the tabloids at a table, and two boys—barely out of college—playing on the solitary slot machine, pints in hand. None of them were paying the pair of them any attention, despite the appreciative glances Andy had received walking in.

Rachel moved her focus back on the girl—the woman—in front of her and prayed to any deity she could name that the words would follow. Rachel wanted to put a palm on her cheek, to still Andy's head as she had her hands. Rachel wanted so much to sooth her, to calm her, to take her into her arms and tell her everything would be okay.

"We've not been to Cuba," Andy pushed on. "You want to go to Cuba?"

"You always found other places for us to go first."

"What if we go this Christmas?"

"I think I need to go by myself, see it for myself rather than through your eyes. Go because I choose it. Not because you finally do."

"We love each other," Andy repeated as her shaking head revealed itself to be crying.

"We do." Rachel nodded, fighting all impulses to wipe away the girl's tears. "But we have different definitions of love, and that's why we need to go separate ways."

Rachel watched as Andy pushed the base of her hand to her eyes, her fingers falling into her fringe. She watched the rise and fall of Andy's chest as she filled her lungs with air, Rachel waited to see what Andy was preparing herself for. The younger woman removed her hands from her eyes and met Rachel's gaze, holding it for a beat before using her wet palms to push down on the table and force herself to stand.

"Okay." She was nodding now, as if resounding herself to the fate. That is how it is. How it must end. "Okay." She looked down at Rachel, still sitting, lukewarm beer back between her hands. Rachel saw her swallow before Andy spoke again. "I'm going to call you though. If I ever want to settle down, I'm calling you."

"You do that." Rachel smiled up at her, only to find Andy bending down, lips meeting in the middle. "Why are you kissing me?" the inevitable question when they finally parted.

"Because I'm not sure when I'll get to do it again." Andy's hand reached out and cupped Rachel's cheek. Where Rachel had been fighting the urge to touch Andy, the younger woman didn't bother. She took what she wanted and acted as she saw fit.

A small touch of Andy's lips to Rachel's temple came next. It was barely there. A ghost of a feeling, fleeting, as if to force Rachel to ask for more. But Rachel kept fighting her impulses. She knew she had to let Andy go. And so, she did. The best friend she met in a Student Union bar all those years ago left Rachel sat in a cold English pub, watching as the door swung closed behind her.

Rachel leant back in her chair and surveyed the group sharing the pub with her, the various men and the solitary barmaid buffing her nails by the till. She looked at her watch, it was barely one pm. It was far too early to be sat in a dark and dank building with this odd collection of people bereft of natural light and anything better to do on a weekday.

She considered her options: returning home to Judi seemed the easiest one, but that would mean answering questions about Andy's impromptu visit and admitting that their unconventional love affair was finally over.

She looked at Andy's untouched glass of red wine, felt the kiss still lingering on her forehead, the scent of Andy's perfume still hanging in the air. Rachel was heavy with fear and doubt. She had loved Andrea Grigoriadis for roughly a third of her life, she wasn't sure how to be Rachel King without her.

Her body was screaming at her to chase after her, to yell, to shout, to tell Andy that she was wrong, she didn't need anything more than Andy was willing to give her, as long as Andy was there Rachel could survive. But she remained rooted to the chair, her limbs weighted down with the realisation that she needed . . .

She didn't have an end to that sentence, to that thought. So finally, she visualised her bank account, and after some quick maths, decided a trip to the phone shop wouldn't be the worst thing in the world before going home and facing her mother.

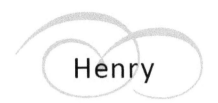

Henry

HIS MOTHER HAD found him lying on his bed, fully clothed, in the dark. The bed hadn't been made, nor had his curtains been opened, when he'd woken that morning. He simply lay on his crumpled covers next to his pyjamas. He'd known she would be coming, he'd heard parts of her conversation with Caitlin through the walls.

Gin.

Questions.

Rose.

Adopt.

Alex.

Weak.

Poorly.

Then it all dropped to a level that even through the thin walls he couldn't hear their conversation.

When she'd knocked, he hadn't answered, so she had waited a cursory couple of seconds before letting herself in. She'd taken in his form, tidied some dirty clothes into his washing basket and moved all his cups into one location near the door before heading for his curtains. He'd watched her, out of the corner of his eye, peer out into the garden below and see the sky darkening before she let the curtains fall back into place.

"I half expected to see your bed sheets tied together and hanging out of the window," she tried to joke, "like one of those bad teen movies you occasionally make me watch."

He'd taken his eyes from his bare ceiling and rolled over to face the wall. He couldn't talk to her, he didn't want to hear what she had to say, but he didn't have the strength of mind to ask her to leave.

He felt the bed move as she sat at its foot.

"Where would you like to start?" she'd asked him and, upon receiving no reply, she'd started at, what he presumed to be, the beginning. It was a story he'd heard countless times before, a story he could recite just as well as his mother, but this time it was no longer the bedtime story he'd grown up with—it was the story of his mother and father and so much more.

Henry didn't go down for supper, nor did he touch the plate of food Caitlin had brought up for him. She had lingered in the doorway, a foot either side of the threshold, as if uncertain of her place.

"If you want to talk," she'd eventually told him, "you know where I am."

But that didn't get a response any more than his mother's words had. He simply lay, staring at the walls.

He had always thought having confirmation of his theories, proof that he had been right, would make him feel better. But knowing that his father had committed suicide just months into Henry's life made him feel so much worse than the uncertainty ever had. Alexander Cole hadn't wanted him any more than Rachel King.

When he no longer heard any movements and was sure the two women were both in their respective beds, he rolled over and found a glass of water had been placed on his nightstand and the untouched meal had been removed, replaced with a simpler sandwich and a packet of crisps.

He'd waited a further couple of hours before he eventually left the safety of his bedroom. He'd checked for signs of life, making sure there weren't any, before he had headed downstairs. His mother's bag was, as it always was, on the bottom stair. He'd found her purse and pulled out her credit card, a subtle cough from the stairs above him allowed him to know he'd been caught.

He thought about defiantly holding on to it, carrying on regardless, but realised how fruitless that endeavour would be. He resigned himself to his fate, replacing the card from where he'd found it before turning around and facing Caitlin. She looked a mess, dressed in some spare clothes of his mother's, hair tussled from sleep, mascara smudged from where she'd failed to take it off before crawling into bed. She was holding an empty glass, he assumed she was on her way to the kitchen.

"Am I in more or less trouble if you're still drunk?" he tried.

"We'll decide that once I hear your explanation." She told him as she passed him and headed through the door to the kitchen. He dug his hands into his pockets and dropped his head, but followed her nonetheless.

He found her heating milk on the hob with the coco out; she was making hot chocolate like his mother did. There were cinnamon sticks and vanilla pods. He half expected to see Nigella Lawson narrating from the side-lines, licking Nutella from a spoon suggestively. He suspected that was one of the reasons Caitlin was doing all of this.

He spotted an empty gin bottle and the crushed plastic of a lemonade bottle waiting to be put out by the backdoor. There was half a bottle of Martini and two glasses by the sink. He was surprised Caitlin was up at all.

He curled up on the sofa and waited for Caitlin to speak to him. When she eventually approached, two cups of steaming cocoa in hand, she nudged at his legs with her foot so he could make room for her to sit beside him.

"What were you planning on buying?"

"Train tickets."

"To?"

"Epping." There was a pause, a furrow of her brow, as if she was trying to figure out the significance of the place. "Rachel's there," he explained for her.

"What happened to Dover?"

"She's split up with her girlfriend. Maybe. I don't know if they were girlfriends, but she's split up from her. If you can—"

"Stop." A hand was placed on his knee. "Your mother and I, or I, would have driven you."

"I know."

"But you didn't want us to?" There was a nod. "Because you're angry with us?" Another nod. "Because you think we lied?"

He shook his head. That wasn't it. His mother never lied to him, Caitlin certainly didn't. But he knew they had both gotten very good at not always telling him the truth.

"I knew about Dad," he eventually confided. "I knew! And yet you two never said. You let me go on thinking—" The hand squeezed his knee, silencing him. Cutting him off once more.

She sipped from her drink, ran her fingers through her hair, pulled her legs up onto the sofa so her feet were off the cold tiles of the floor. He watched every action and waited for her to speak.

"You've always asked about your dad, you've no doubt bombarded Rachel with a bunch of questions about her these past few days. Have you ever asked about your mum?"

What was there to ask? He'd grown up with her, he knew everything there was to know. Most of their lives it had just been the two of them, them against the world. How could he not know her?

"I met your mum at school. She'd come from the prep school down the road. I fell in love with her instantly. There was something about her. Something incredible. She has so much fire. So much passion. Even then I knew, I knew that she was the woman for me and that I would do anything for her." Though the kitchen was dimly lit, Caitlin's eyes shone. Henry wasn't sure what they were shining with, he couldn't tell if this was a happy story or a sad one. "Her mother, your grandmother, wasn't quite so convinced. She didn't say anything hateful, nothing derogatory, no names were called, but it was clear that she didn't approve. She said things like 'it will be a harder life', and 'I don't mind but others might', or 'it's not the life I would choose for you'. The one that finally persuaded your mum though was 'I thought you wanted a family', and she did. All your mum ever spoke about was the son she'd have and how she would love him. Your grandmother convinced her that she would never be able to have that with me."

Henry put his cup down on the small table in front of them and curled up into her waiting embrace. Her arm, covered in goose bumps from the frigid night air of the old kitchen, warmed him.

"That's not to say I gave up though. I suggested we go to St Andrews for university. That in Scotland we would be far away from her mother and we would be free to build that life that we'd spoken about countless nights laying beside each other, staring up at the ceiling."

"She met Dad at university."

"She met your father." She nodded beside him, her arm still tightly wrapped around his slender frame. "He was in front of a table preaching about the SNP; he had this all-encompassing presence, this aura that drew her to him. She fell for that man so fast, so strong, that it surpassed anything she felt for me. The fact that he was a man was irrelevant. He could have been anything and she would still have loved him. Don't get me wrong," she nuzzled into his hair, "I think approval from your grandmother and the fact he could give her children helped tremendously. But it was him she ultimately fell for."

"What about you?"

"I joined a Gay and Lesbian society at university and met other like-minded people. I met women with shaved heads and hairy armpits, women with purple lipstick, vegans, Jews, Pagans, I even dated the daughter of two vicars for a while—she made your mother's issues look like a non-starter." She laughed. "The point is that I met all these women and I discovered that it's okay: I'm just me, like your mum is just her and your dad was just your dad, and

Rachel is just Rachel, and you are going to be whoever you want to be."

"Do you still love Mum?"

"I will always love your mother."

"But you love Matt too?" Henry moved away from her, out of her arms, so he could properly look into her face. "Is that why you didn't have children? Because you love Mum?"

"No, my dear boy," she pulled him back in close to her, "I simply couldn't, and Matt didn't want to carry. I mean, could you imagine a pregnant Matt?"

He thought about it for a minute, trying to picture Matt's strong figure with a pregnancy bump. "I guess not. But why didn't you adopt?"

"In 2002 they changed the adoption laws, allowing non-married people to adopt children. The government made it very clear that it wasn't a Gay Rights thing, but people didn't fail to notice that queer couples could take advantage. However, by that point Matt was already working in Brussels and I didn't want to raise a child by myself. Anyway," she nudged him playfully in the ribs, "I had you to contend with. You were enough for me."

Henry thought about Caitlin's words for a moment, he placed them in line next to the words Rachel had said to him the day before. We just happen to have more parents than other people.

He burrowed himself back in next to her. "I love you."

"And I love you, Hen," a tender kiss was placed on his crown, "like your mum loves you, like your dad did, like Matt does."

"Do you think Rachel might?"

"If you want to form a relationship with her and she feels able to form one with you, I have no doubt that she will love you too."

"Okay." He nodded into her nook before pushing himself up and away from her once more. "I'm going to wake Mum up."

"She'll be thrilled, no doubt." He heard Caitlin sigh to his retreating form.

Elizabeth

SHE NEVER SLEPT well when she'd been drinking. The fact that she could hear Caitlin and Henry banging about downstairs was not helping. Nor the cycle of memories circling her mind. She'd thought about getting up and joining them. From the sounds of the metallic ringing, Caitlin was making something on the hob, probably hot chocolate; where most people craved grease when they'd been drinking, Caitlin's sweet tooth rose to the surface. She'd become a master of drunk baking brownies, though the time she'd confused baking soda with the tiny container of corn flower hadn't been her finest moment.

The tradition had started sometime in the early nineties. Caitlin had arrived on her doorstep in Fife, at the point of inebriation that only sleep could remedy. Elizabeth had folded her arms across her chest and refused admittance to her best friend, but Caitlin had argued that she was far too drunk and pathetic to be sent away. Alex had offered to drive her home, but in the ten minutes it had taken him to locate his car keys, Caitlin had broken down in tears, confessed her affair with the mathematics professor, and promised she hadn't realised she was *Elizabeth's* mathematics professor until she'd seen Elizabeth's paper waiting to be marked as she'd searched for her bra in the older woman's room.

Elizabeth had looked up at Alex leaning against the doorframe, keys dangling from his fingers as he threw on a jacket, Caitlin sobbing into her jumper. She agreed that Caitlin was too drunk and pathetic to be sent away into the night. Alex had dropped his keys on the coffee table, shrugged his jacket off and cast it away onto the back of a chair with a promise to return with pillows and blankets.

The next time was after they'd all graduated, she and Alex had moved to London, Caitlin had followed. The Spice Girls were on the television and once again Caitlin was standing with finger pressed unrelentingly against the buzzer to the flat, demanding entrance. Elizabeth had called out of the window to the girl below, finger still firmly pressed against the buzzer, and told her to go home because she was drunk. *I'm not drunk, I'm in love,* Caitlin had called back up to her. *Your love smells like gin and menthols.* Elizabeth had acceded though, much to Alex's chagrin, and allowed her up. Caitlin proceeded to tell them both about a dinner she had just had with a woman named Mattilda, opening wine for them all, not noticing that she was the only one drinking.

Though it was subtler now, the drunken sleepovers had become more frequent since Matt had taken the job in Brussels. Caitlin would have one too many glasses of wine with dinner or stop by unannounced and demand that Elizabeth share the bottle a grateful cat owner had given her in addition to payment. A couple of times, when it first started, Elizabeth had offered Caitlin the spare room before she got too drunk to drive, however, on those occasions Caitlin had insisted that she go home, that people were entrusting her with their cats, she should probably supervise them. Elizabeth soon realised that Caitlin didn't want Elizabeth to offer her a bed for the night, that Caitlin didn't want her to notice how lonely she was, that Caitlin needed to pretend, that she needed the pretence of being unable to get home.

The two of them had fallen into a sort of rhythm with each other. Alex hadn't cared for it and it had taken Matt a while to adjust, but Caitlin was always going to be a feature of Elizabeth's life, just as she was always going to be a part of Caitlin's.

It suddenly seemed so natural that it would be Caitlin that her son was downstairs talking to. The same way that it was Caitlin he'd gone to when he'd first started going out with Alyssa, that it was Caitlin that had provided him with condoms, and it was Caitlin he had confided in the first (and hopefully last) time he'd smoked pot.

She heard feet ascending the stairs; from the heaviness of the footfall she reasoned it was Henry. A moment later the light was on in the hallway and her door was pushed, somewhat haphazardly, open. She saw Henry standing in the doorway, a hot cup of something or other in each hand as he returned his right foot to the ground.

"I do wish you wouldn't kick open doors."

"You're awake." He beamed at her as he trundled further into her room.

"And you seem to be in a good mood, what happened to the maudlin teenager that wouldn't speak to me?" She sat up and took the hot chocolate that had been left for her on her bedside unit, as Henry walked round to the other side of her bed.

"Caitlin made him hot chocolate!"

"Caitlin laced it with Baileys." She sighed, but sipped from it nonetheless.

"So," Henry relaxed into the pillows next to her and Elizabeth waited her son to announce the reason for his midnight calling, "Caitlin was talking to me about you."

"This bodes well," she placed her cup on the nightstand and wrapped an arm around him, "And just what was it that she was saying?"

"Just stuff about you, her, and Dad."

"Your vagueness does not alleviate my sense of foreboding, my precious little man."

"Why did you choose Dad over her?"

The question had her sit up straighter and a couple of hairs prickled on the back of her neck. She reached for her cup again, hoping that the movement would distract her. "I didn't think I was choosing at the time," she eventually whispered out into the night.

"I—"

"I thought I might be able to have them both," she clarified, before Henry could tell her that he didn't understand. "And in a way, I did. I had your father and I had my best friend. I had the love of them both and they had mine."

"How come you've had boyfriends since Dad died, but not girlfriends?"

She thought about his question, considered all the answers she might be able to give him. Thought about a night when Henry was seven or eight, when Matt was away in Brussels, when she and Caitlin had been lying on the sofa and Henry had fallen asleep on the floor in front of them, the remnants of one of his Disney films still playing on the television. She thought about the feel of Caitlin's body next to hers, the sound of her son softly snoring, the warmth of home surrounding her.

The sudden weight of her son on her shoulder brought her back to the night, brought her back to the now. She removed the cup from his loosening grip and placed it besides her own on the bedside table. Before wrapping an arm around him and gently waking him back up.

"Come on little man," she soothed as he stirred, "time to go back to bed."

He rubbed at his eyes as she guided him into a seated position, a kiss to her cheek and he was off again. Feet gently trudging behind him as he sailed off back to his room. She watched as lights flipped off and listened as his door caught on the carpet as he pushed it closed.

When she heard his bed groan with her son's weight, she got out of her own, pulled on her dressing gown and headed downstairs with the two empty cups, relieved that she had a few more hours to be able to formulate an answer to her son's question.

Caitlin was talking softly on the phone as she entered the

kitchen, the gentle exchanges she could hear of two people that knew each other inside and out let Elizabeth know it was Matt, despite the fact that it was even later in the morning in Belgium, that Caitlin was speaking with.

Caitlin looked up and saw her, a smile and a wave, as she tidied up her telephone conversation with her partner of nearly two decades, and then she was standing beside Elizabeth, helping her with the washing up.

"When will you accept that woman's proposal?"

"You know when," Caitlin answered simply, drying up the pan she'd just been passed.

"It's not like you even want to get married in Northern Ireland."

"It's the principle."

"She won't wait forever."

"She's waited this long, a little longer won't hurt her."

"What if it hurts you?"

"She's waited this long," Caitlin repeated, taking the last item to be dried from Elizabeth. "You should be asleep," she finished, passing the wooden spoon back so Elizabeth could put it away.

"It's," a quick glance to the clock on the wall, "coming up for four, I think I'm passed sleep."

"What about work?"

"I'll quit." Elizabeth smiled at her, to which she received a raised eyebrow. "I'll muddle through, I always do." The smile was replaced with a shrug. "It won't be my first working day on the back of no sleep. It's all part of motherhood."

"I'll take Hen back to Sevenoaks with me, we'll relieve Astrid from the cat poo, and you'll join us after work. We could go riding if the evening holds."

None of it was a suggestion, none of it had to be.

Elizabeth has started to put away the bits and pieces Caitlin had picked out to make the hot chocolate. When she got the cupboard with the paracetamol, Elizabeth threw a sheet at her.

Elizabeth watched the woman before her. Caitlin's hair was all over the place, a mixture of the little sleep she'd had and the previous day's product. She was wearing some branded clothes Elizabeth had bought when she'd joined a gym, but never worn and the membership never used. Caitlin's eyes were dark, a horrible combination of yesterday's makeup and tired bags sagging beneath them.

Elizabeth wondered if Caitlin would hate her as much as Henry would, when they both realised how selfish she'd been. The boy growing up without his father because Elizabeth had insisted upon a child. The woman living in half a marriage because Elizabeth had been determined to have it all.

Rachel

HALFWAY THROUGH THE second day of her stay in Epping, Rachel found Judi in the kitchen standing over the ironing board with a pile of clothes, one neater than the other, on either side of her. Rachel placed a kiss on her cheek as she skirted round her to the kettle.

"Tea?" she asked as she sorted out a cup of coffee for herself and listened to Judi hum her response. "Where's Rob?"

"The allotment."

"When did he get so old man?"

She looked through the fridge for something to eat, and having already pilfered a handful of grapes, settled on a yoghurt.

"Leave him be, he's seventy-one, let him have his courgettes."

Judi put the shirt she was ironing on a hanger and rested it on the back of one of the kitchen chairs. She met Rachel at the counter, grasping her freshly made cup of tea between two hands.

"Not that I don't love you being here, but how long are you planning on staying?" Rachel pulled out a folded piece of paper from her back pocket and placed it on the countertop between them. Judi swapped her cup for the freshly produced piece of paper. "'Visit to Cuba. Sort shit out. Meet a woman'," she read from it.

Rachel smiled her agreement at its content and took the paper back, pinning it under a magnet to the fridge.

1. *Visit Cuba.*
2. *Sort shit out. Job? House? Location?*

3.   Meet a ~~girl~~ woman.

Her messy handwriting on an old sheet of Tottenham Hotspur notelet paper looked out of place between a photograph of Tom with his new family and Luke with his, yet it seemed just as monumental to her.

"And your job?" Judi mused.

"If I negotiate a reduced redundancy on the agreement, I could leave now."

"You said you didn't know what was happening with work."

"Technically true."

To avoid eye contact she found a sudden interest in finding a teaspoon for her yoghurt. "I didn't know if I would take one of the redundancies, thus I did not know what was happening at work."

"How reduced?"

"Couple of grand."

"I don't like how nonchalant you sound about all of this."

"I have no dependents, no car, my rent was reasonable and split with Andy—"

"Was?"

"Was." She nodded, washing up her spoon and rinsing out her pot and placing it with the recycling. "I have money in the bank. I've got my visa and flights sorted, if you can put up with me for a month, I'll spend the end of November out there and be back for Christmas. Then I'll sort my life out in the New Year."

Rachel smiled.

"And do what?"

"I've looked into doing a master's degree at LSE."

Judi folded her arms over her chest. Rachel watched her close her eyes and could almost hear the silent count to ten in the woman's head. Judi always composed herself before she spoke, rarely allowing her words to pour out on instinct. Rob, however, spoke first and thought afterwards. She didn't know how he had managed to lead classrooms of noisy teenagers for all those years. Of her two parents, she often thought Judi was more suited to teaching, having the patience of mind to deal the impetuous nature of secondary school children. Yet Judi, like any good baby boomer, stayed at home to raise the children while her husband went out to work.

"And what triggered all of this?" Judi eventually voiced.

"Henry was in my room." She shrugged, picking up her black coffee, hoping it was cool enough to drink. "He saw my posters of Cuba, asked if I'd ever been." Another shrug. "Asked what I wanted to be when I grew up."

"And?"

"I realised two things."

Rachel moved over to the table, emptying one of the chairs of its freshly ironed clothes, she sat down opposite the fruit bowl and started toying with an orange.

"I've yet to grow up."

"And the other thing?" Judi pressed, taking the orange from her and placing it back with the rest of the fruit.

"I made a massive decision when I was seventeen and I haven't made one since."

She took her bottom lip between her teeth. She needn't have looked across at Judi to know her brow was knitted as she carefully constructed sentences to lead them forwards. She knew it would take Judi a while, so she ploughed forward herself:

"I've been coasting. Finding people to make choices for me to avoid making any of my own, sort of bumbling along, hoping that life would just land at my feet."

"How do you mean?" Judi was sitting beside her now, the un-ironed clothes moved back into the hamper, so she could sit with her at the table.

"You and Rob enrolled me into college and found me A Levels to take. It was there I met Rebecca and she decided we were going to go to Sussex. Aidan then told me to redo it all, found me Kent, where I met Andy and I've been doing whatever she suggests ever since." She took the orange back from the bowl and dug into it with the tip of her nail, the acidity of its juice cutting into the sensitive skin underneath. She didn't want to eat the fruit, just desperately found herself in need of something to do with her hands. Judi's intense gaze was making her feel uneasy, causing her to fidget in her seat.

"I think I've been using her." She ventured a look up at the older woman and found Judi opening and closing her mouth. "What?"

"Of all the things I was expecting, that was not it."

Judi bit into an orange of her own to break its skin before adding her own peelings to Rachel's neat pile.

"I know you and Rob don't like her."

They were separating the segments now, but neither were eating.

"You can only watch someone hurt your daughter so many times."

"I've been waiting for Andy for, what? A decade?"

Rachel looked across at Judi for confirmation of her estimate and was rewarded with a tight nod.

"But, I think, all the time I've been holding out for her to commit to me, and me alone, I've actually been using her as an excuse to not live my life."

Segments separated, they began working on the pith, tiny strings of white being added to the tower of peel between them.

"Like I had a chance at a family with Daniel, but I gave it away."

"You were seventeen and you *are* very much a lesbian. You couldn't have had a family with him, it would have killed you."

"Not in the heteronormative, Daniel would come home from work to dinner on the table and a doting wife, sense. But in the, we could have co-parented, every other weekend and all the Jewish holidays, sense."

"Neither of you are Jewish."

"It's a phrase."

Picture perfect orange sections were being stacked together to reform their hemispheres.

"It's not a phrase."

"Could be a phrase."

She popped a piece of fruit into her mouth, holding it between tongue and teeth, increasing the pressure slightly, and the juice spilled out and ran down the back of her throat.

"Oh my God!"

Rachel spat the decimated mouthful into her hand.

"How old is this orange?"

The sticky mess slid from hand to table, the fruit and peelings were pushed away, palm wiped on her trousers and coffee nestled back between her two hands. The residual juice of the orange meeting the warmth of the mug.

"Henry's a good kid, Elizabeth's a good mum: they're a good family. It's time I stopped feeling guilty and find one of my own."

"And Andy?"

"She's nobody's wife."

She kept her head bowed over her coffee but looked up at Judi, a small smile on her lips.

"Everyone deserves to be happy."

"Everyone?"

"Maybe not everyone," Judi corrected with a roll of her eyes. "Crazed dictators and people on the dark net aside, everyone else deserves to be happy. You've waited too long to be happy."

Rachel nodded her agreement and tidied away the mess of the table before heading back upstairs to her laptop.

Her pillows had been moved so her back could be pressed rigidly against the headboard, laptop resting on top of the inside of her thighs as her fingers danced across its keys, flicking between tabs on the internet, continuing her research into her fortnight in Cuba, when Judi came in with a new cup of coffee for her.

"What do you mean guilty?" she asked, putting the drink down on her bedside table as she sat down beside her.

Rachel closed her computer and gently dropped it on the floor. "What?"

"Earlier, you said it was time you stopped feeling guilty."

She smiled to herself, knowing Judi had been working out the perfect way to phrase the previously asked question.

"Do you feel guilty for giving Henry away?"

"Kinda, but mainly I feel guilty about Daniel."

Rachel took the drink in her hand and looked across at Judi beside her, legs stretched out and crossed at the ankles.

"You know my feelings on family, but that doesn't shake the dichotomy that Daniel has a child he doesn't know about."

She sipped from her drink, before resting it where her laptop had been perched on her knees.

"He adored me, and I repaid him by using him to answer a question I knew the answer to, getting knocked up and then making a life-changing decision without him. I'm as Women's Choice as they come, but when I found out I was pregnant it wasn't a foetus any more, it was a baby and I chose what to do with it. I chose to give it away. I didn't want it, but I didn't want Daniel to have it either. If the O'Reillys reacted any way like you and Rob did, they would have helped Daniel raise it, yet I didn't let him have that option."

Her soliloquy over, she looked back to Judi. "Who does a child belong to?"

"Ergo: guilt."

They sat in silence, each holding their cups of coffee tightly between their hands.

"Do you ever think about reaching out to your birth mother?"

Rachel passed across her coffee for Judi to hold and rose quickly from the bed, she located her bag, and pulled Henry's folder from beneath the child's football shirt. Sitting back beside Judi, she swapped her history for her cup.

"Henry found her. My dad, this Matthew King, died in Northern Ireland while it was still really bad over there. My mum, Annabelle, gave me up like a year later."

"This all matches us with your files from the social workers. I dread to think how Henry got all this." Judi leafed through the boy's research. "If doctors had known more about post-natal depression, if she'd received more help, I would never have got you," she murmured as she thumbed the pages. "I'm a wretched person for being grateful for her misery."

Rachel moved closer to her and placed her head on her shoulder. "I know you're my mum."

"Do you want to meet her?"

"Most of the time, no. She had her chance to be my mum and she didn't want it. She left me in foster care, she could have come back at any time, but she didn't. She chose to leave me, to move on." Rachel swallowed whatever feelings were developing in her throat. "She knew where I was, but she left me."

Judi snaked an arm around her back and held her closer, dropping her head onto her own after laying a tender kiss on her temple.

"Then there are other days, not even days, moments really. Always fleeting, and usually when I'm brushing my teeth—looking at my reflection—I want to know. I want to talk to her, find out if she's got a weird birth mark on her side too, or if she gets—got?—really irritable during her period as well, or if the reason my jaw clicks when I eat is something to do with her genes."

"What stops you?"

"What if she's nice? What if I like her and we get on?"

"Would that be so terrible?"

"Yes." Rachel's throat was tight, her chest painful, her eyes heavy from the tears she was holding back. "She can't be nice. I can't like her. She's not my mum. You raised me, you loved me, you continue to let me live here—rent free," she looked up from Judi's shoulder, the beginnings of a smile on her lips. "If I need a kidney, then maybe I'll hunt her down."

"What about Henry?"

"He should probably save his kidneys for his own kids."

Judi shrugged her shoulder, forcing Rachel to sit up and take the conversation seriously. "You know what I mean."

"He'll realise soon enough that he has all the mum he needs in Elizabeth."

"And now we get to the truth as to why you're hiding in your bedroom again."

Rachel looked across at her mother to find her face hidden behind that knowing smile she always seemed to wear.

"He's going to leave you."

Rachel couldn't tell what face she was pulling, but she assumed it must have been somewhat pitiful as her mother drew her in closer to her.

"He's not, but that's what you think is going to happen. So, you're hiding away from him, from Elizabeth—she's lovely by the way—from Andy and from life, so none of them can find you."

She leaned into her mother's hug and considered what she was being told.

"Look," once again Judi moved so Rachel was forced to sit back up, "he took the effort to find you, to find out about you." The paper-thin folder of Rachel's birth parents was gestured at. "What makes you think he's just going to disappear now he's here, now he's met you?"

"It wasn't me he was looking for, it was his father. His adoptive father, not birth," Rachel clarified, once again realising just how many parents she and Henry had between them.

"But it's you that he's found."

"Because his father is dead."

Judi frowned at her.

"Elizabeth's husband died when Henry was baby, Henry

222

implied—or I inferred, I can never remember the difference—that it was suicide. He thinks Elizabeth will 'return' him if he's sad too."

"You know, you don't stop being vulnerable just because you're over the age of eighteen."

"Hen—"

"Not Henry, you." It was Rachel's turn to frown now, as she tried to work out what it was her Judi was trying to tell her. "How about, instead of running off to Cuba, you talk to them."

"And say what?"

"I think that's for you to decide, my darling girl."

Henry

CAITLIN USUALLY DROVE them back the long way, down the B roads and country lanes, passed quaint village pubs and through wooded areas, where it was more tree than tarmac, how Henry imagined it would have been years ago. Not today though. Caitlin was speeding down the M25 as if she were being chased. A couple of times, Henry worried they were, as she was overtaking and undercutting other drivers, but as her swearing increased and her impatience with the rest on the road vanished to nothing, he realised she was just trying to escape last night. Put as much distance between them as she could.

Henry had tried to talk to Caitlin about his mum's mood, of course he had, he'd got as far as *Hey, what's up with mu*—before Caitlin had sounded her buzzer and turned the music up on the radio. So, Henry alternated the journey back to the house between staring out of the window and messaging Alyssa.

Yesterday morning he was woken by Caitlin bringing him in a cup of tea, it was placed on his bedside table as she drew open the curtains. Once light was in the room, he could see clearly that she'd chosen his favourite Star Wars mug to wake him; sitting up and sipping from it he found it was just to his liking—two sugars, with more milk than tea.

Thirty minutes and we're off, he was told before Caitlin departed.

As soon as he was showered and dressed, he was whisked off

back to Sevenoaks and put to work in the cattery, before sitting with Thatcher as Caitlin attended to her horses. They'd made supper from scratch, getting messy as they mixed dough for pizza bases, Caitlin flicking flour at him as she smiled.

You mother likes it when we do pompously middle-class things like this.

You are pompously middle-class.

I'll have you know there isn't a single avocado in the house.

You have artichokes in your fridge, three horses, and your dog is named Thatcher.

More flour was flicked at him and more mess was made. He was chased around the kitchen to cries of *ironically*, and *Matt named him*.

When his mother walked into Caitlin's house a couple of hours later, she was greeted with a glass of wine pressed into her hand and instructions to *sit, eat, and be merry*. As he and Caitlin continued to chatter around the table, devouring the pizza they had made, he noticed that his mother barely said a word. Caitlin took her out riding and he was left to the washing up, they returned to him flicking through the movie channels on Caitlin's Sky box.

His mother had kissed him on the cheek and told him to gather his things. He'd looked to Caitlin and she'd wrapped an arm around his mother, sweeping her to the sofa.

"Watch a film with us," he'd heard her whisper. "If you still want to go afterwards, I'll plaster you with wine."

"Caity." Her name was slow and deliberate on his mother's lips. The same way she'd pronounce his when he was testing her limits. The last time his name had been said like that he'd been negotiating a £15 'loan' into a £20.

"Just watch a film with us," Caitlin had replied in the same way Henry had managed to close the deal at £30.

He'd chosen, what he deemed to be at least, a harmless weather apocalypse drama. Caitlin had complained as if Al Gore had directed

Happy Feet.

Who's Al Gore?

His mother said nothing.

The man who should have got the presidency instead of George Bush.

Who's George Bush?

Still his mother said nothing.

His mother said nothing as her wine glass was refilled, a couple too many times. His mother said nothing as he and Caitlin started to play *Mario Kart* on Matt's barely touched Wii.

It wasn't until they all went to bed, and Caitlin had kissed her on the cheek as his mother made her way into the larger guest bedroom, did Henry suddenly realise why.

His thoughts went back to that Sunday morning, to coming downstairs to Sam sprawled out on the floor surrounded by scatterings of the morning paper, his mother sat high against the edge of the sofa reading to him.

His mother didn't enjoy playing happy families any more than he did.

His mother had spent the whole evening looking at a life that could have been hers had she not chosen his father over Caitlin. Perhaps Henry would be blonder in that life. Perhaps he might not be Henry at all.

He could be Henrietta.

A Charlotte.

He might be older or younger. It wouldn't be him in that house. It might not even be that house. He didn't know if Caitlin chose it or Matt. Perhaps his mother and Caitlin might live in Surrey with their child. To be closer to her parents. They might have stayed in Scotland. Moved to Edinburgh or farther north.

Without his mother to adopt him, he might have remained baby King. Or Rachel might have found somebody else to love him. Maybe she wouldn't have. Couldn't have. He might have been like Grace, a timeline ever lengthening without his mother's love to tether him to one place.

Thatcher whined from the backseat. Henry felt like joining in.

It was done, it was over.

He had met his birth mother.

He'd had it confirmed that his father committed suicide.

Everything was tied up in a neat little bow, he just needed to work out what to do with it all. And yet his bones ached with the weight of it all. He didn't understand how they could feel heavy and hollow at the same time. He didn't understand how he could feel them at all. It started pulling at his throat, like something was hanging on to his Adam's Apple. This bulk held him down yet managed to make him feel like he could float away at the same time. He had this duality about him that he couldn't reconcile.

He turned the radio off and tried to focus on Caitlin. They were pulling into the village now. If he didn't start her talking soon, they would be out of the car. She would have the whole house to avoid his questions. She might even drop him off and return to the sanctuary of her own home.

"You don't get to decide what I do and don't get to know," he told her, his old primary school passing them by in a haze of colours as Caitlin continued to speed through their journey.

"And if I don't know the answers?" She dropped the car into second, preparing to take the final turning to the farm house.

"But you do know, you know why mum's being weird too, you just don't want to admit it."

"I don't know what you mean."

"She was fine, she was okay at the very least, and then yesterday she wigged out about something, and given that last Wednesday my birth mother had to call her to get her to pick me up from her flat in Dover, I think that's saying a lot!"

"Li—"

But it was too late. Henry had been too slow to push Caitlin into answers, they'd pulled up into the drive and not only would Caitlin be able to escape from the car and his questions, she now had something else to distract him with. That something was parked where Sam's car usually resided.

"Can Alyssa drive?"

"No." Henry frowned, looking towards the VW Camper for answers. "But if this is her way of telling me she's passed her test, I'm all in."

"I'm pretty sure this is a teen pregnancy waiting to happen in that case." Caitlin sighed, climbing out of the car and opening the door for Thatcher to do the same.

Henry was already at the van and peering in, its height was only a foot or so taller than himself and he could easily see though the aged windows of the classic vehicle. As Caitlin came to stand beside him, her back bent where she was trying to maintain hold of Thatcher's collar. Henry turned and pressed a finger upright against his lips and then took the dog from Caitlin so she, too, could see Rachel, headphones in, curled up and sleeping on one of the benches.

"Who?" she mouthed at him.

"Rachel." He smiled.

"The birth mother?" She frowned back, receiving a simple nod. She took Thatcher back from him before saying, "You wake her up. I better call your mum and let her know of this new development."

"Why?"

"Why do you need to wake her up or why do I need to call your mum?"

"Mum."

"This is the kind of thing she would want to know about. Your birth mother can't just show up unannounced, especially not in a camper van."

"Why not?"

Caitlin suddenly looked very tired. As if she had barely slept these pasts few days either. Like she'd shared all of his mother's worries, like this whole adventure had been just as stressful for her too. Like Henry had more parents than other people.

She adjusted her grip on the dog, crouching down beside him so that he might be more amenable to being held in place.

"She signed away her parental rights, Hen," Caitlin said softly looking up at him from the ground, "she can't just turn up like this. She's a stranger. It's weird. Finding her sleeping in a camper van, however cool it might be, is weirder still."

"But—"

"When you're eighteen you can make these decisions for yourself, but until then, your mum has to make them. She'll still want to make them once you're eighteen, probably up until the day she dies, but for now, legally, you have no say in the matter."

"But I'm allowed to wake her up?"

"I doubt, very much, you're going to agree to going inside and pretending she's not here."

He passed her his house key and waited for the woman and dog to be firmly behind the front door before he opened the side door to the camper. As he climbed in, Rachel rearranged herself so she was sat neatly at one of the benches and pointed at the other for Henry.

"How much did you hear?"

"How much do you want me to have heard?"

"None."

"In which case." She feigned a yawn and made an elaborate show of stretching her arms and back, rolling her head along her shoulders for good measures.

"Caitlin's just protective."

Rachel threw an arm over the back of her seat and watched the house. From where Henry was sitting, he could see through the kitchen windows, meaning Rachel could see better still. She would be able to see Caitlin, landline pressed tightly against her face, mouthing words that would be like, *She's here* or, *Do you want me to call the police?* She might now be on the phone to Matt, interrupting her working day, seeking advice from someone more impartial. The perspective of someone slightly less involved.

"She and Mum have been friends since school. Matt works in Belgium. I think she's a politician or something. She's met Nigel Farage. And a David Someone."

"And Matt is?"

"Caitlin's girlfriend."

"I thought me being gay made your mum a bit uneasy," Rachel said slowly as she turned back to face him. "You know, the way she shut dinner down the other night."

"Caitlin says it's because Mum's Anglican, that there's all this stuff she finds difficult to talk about."

"I get that," she nodded, "I do."

Henry had thought he'd *got that* too. He'd spent much of last night, while he was trying to sleep, thinking about how he got *that*. Considering the life of a child that could have been him, but could never have been him, that had his mum and Caitlin for parents. He thought about the life that his mum had tried to build without his father. He thought about the life Caitlin had built without his mother. He thought he'd got *that*.

Sitting opposite Rachel in a dusty old camper van, her arrival as unexplained as the classic car, he no longer thought he had *that*. That seemed to be very far away.

Elizabeth

IT SEEMED SO fitting that the phone call would come on a Wednesday.

It had been a week, after all. The symmetry of it all was beautiful. Poetic even.

She mapped out the past week in her head. Renamed all of the days to fit the life event that day brought.

Wednesday became Dover.

Thursday became Pyjamas.

Friday became Dinner.

Saturday to Sam. Sam's day. Samsday. Samedi. She liked that. She liked that a lot.

Sunday would become Epping.

Monday to—she didn't know what to rename Monday to. She could feel herself crumbling on the edge of the guest bed. Felt the coarseness of the hem of the cotton pillow as she fiddled with it. The strangeness of the words as they were said aloud. *Henry was too much for him.*

Monday got its name from the moon. It did in most European languages.

Alex, a century before his death, might have been labelled a lunatic. Sixteen years later he might still be dubbed such a thing by some.

She wobbled about in her desk chair. Its casters pulling slowly against the thin shag of the commercial carpet.

They used to spin lunatics. Spin them round and round. Faster and faster.

The motion was meant to propel the madness out of them.

Henry was too much for him.

Perhaps Monday would remain Monday.

Tuesday was named after Tiw. Tiw was a one-handed Norse god of combat. On the continent Tuesday got its name from Mars, the Roman God of War. That felt fitting too. The war going on inside her head. The battle she had between wanting everyone to know it all. To have the truth laid out. But to have everything remain the same. To have everyone to continue to love her. The battle of her selfishness, her cowardice, and her constant need for Henry to be protected. To be loved. To be the most loved little man in the world and for him to love her in return.

Perhaps Tuesday could remain as well.

She looked down at the ledger, usually it just bore numbers. Long division. Simple multiplication. Long lists of numbers to be stacked together and made one. Calculations that she either didn't need a calculator for or didn't trust a calculator with. She worked mainly on Excel, but old habits die hard. There was something soothing about doing the maths herself. She liked that numbers were always the same.

Almost universal. There was no language when it came to numerals.

Today her ledger had words on. The white of the paper dampened with her handwriting. Her notes on her personal week.

Wednesday Dover
Thursday Pyjamas
Friday Dinner
Saturday ~~Sam~~ ~~Samsday~~ SAMEDI
Sunday Epping
Monday

Tuesday

She crossed out 'Dover' and replaced it with 'Rachel'.

Of course, the phone call would come on a Wednesday. It had last week.

* * *

Parking at her house was getting cramped.

The farmhouse was much too large for just Henry and herself. It was so large that an entire other person moved in and she hadn't noticed. She looked at the two other cars in her driveway and thought about how life might have been.

The other day it had been Sam's Land Rover parked next to Caitlin's Mini. Today there was the VW camper—yellow monstrosity that clashed violently with the surroundings autumn gave them.

She'd looked into cars for Henry. Though he was a while away from seventeen, she knew he would want driving lessons for his birthday. She'd been looking into cars for him. He wouldn't be learning in her Audi. It might only be a family car, it might be approaching its fifth year, but it was still much too powerful for him.

She'd sought advice from Caitlin, flicked through Auto Trader on the iPad, and they'd settled on a Škoda. She couldn't remember the exact model, but she had a tab open on her phone devoted to it.

She pictured the Škoda, it would be red like Henry's beloved Arsenal, on her driveway. She looked at the two vehicles already there. Sam's Land Rover wasn't missing from the picture. Nor, she found herself realising, was Alex's Ford Escort.

There would never be another Ford on her drive.

She checked her reflection in the rear-view mirror, poked at her eyes and pulled down the bags from under them just to have them slowly crawl back up when she let go. She found some concealer within the depths of her handbag and tried to hide the worst of it. Ran fingers through her hair, trying to find some volume at this late stage of the day.

Dropping everything back into her bag, she noted the time on her phone. Rachel's VW had been camped on her drive for at least three hours now. She wondered what they would all be discussing inside. Not wanting to dwell on the possibilities, she gave herself a final once over before stepping out the car and into her house.

Her home.

Having slipped out of her heels and coat, and dropped her handbag on the bottom stair, she found the three of them in the living room. The television was on, Henry had them watching *The Simpsons*, but she doubted any of them could tell her what the episode was about.

Thatcher dutifully crept down from the sofa and sank low onto the floor as if to pretend he had been there, beside Henry, all along. The rest of them all looked to her, all of them asking what was to happen next.

Elizabeth thought back to the meal of shepherd's pie that no one really ate, to Rachel's awkwardness sat on the wooden chair in the ever-cold kitchen. Elizabeth found herself relating to Rachel's unease. She'd told her that she'd invited her to supper so she could provide her son, their son, with answers.

But with three sets of eyes now looking up at her, Elizabeth felt that there might not be anything worse than not having the answers.

Rachel

CAITLIN SAID GOODBYE barely moments after Elizabeth had said hello. The woman had left with a kiss to Elizabeth's cheek and another to Henry's forehead. Rachel had watched it all from her position on the sofa, studied how the two women had interacted and the fondness Caitlin clearly had for Henry.

He was so loved.

Henry had reached out to Rachel, worried that he might be returned, as he'd phrased it. He had hunted her down to find out more about where he had come from to make sure he could stay with his adoptive mother. Make sure he was good enough for Elizabeth.

Little did Henry understand that nothing in the world would separate Elizabeth from him.

Nothing.

"Would you like a drink? Wine? Beer? Tea or coffee?"

"Coffee sounds good." Rachel accepted, looking for the now empty mug that Caitlin had given her earlier. "I'll help you."

By the time Rachel had located her cup and met Elizabeth in the kitchen, the kettle was already on to boil and a glass of wine was being poured.

"Why are you here?" she was asked, Elizabeth's back still to her.

Henry had asked that. Though the harshness of his tone was the same, it managed to lack the coolness of Elizabeth's delivery. Rachel had been sure of the answer when Henry asked, she wanted to speak with Elizabeth, but now—with Elizabeth asking the question—she wasn't so sure. It was Elizabeth that she once again wanted to speak to, Elizabeth was once again the reason for her visit. Yet, she wasn't as sure in her convictions this time around.

Previously she thought her visit was a means to an end.

This time she wanted more and that was harder to cope with. She seldom wanted more. Rachel had always been so happy with anything that was offered to her—her decade-long friendship with Andy was testament to that fact—yet here she was asking for more, and Elizabeth was now Mr Bumble and Rachel was just another orphan in that Dickensian novel she'd tried so hard to distance herself from.

The question was, was she asking for more of Henry, or more of both him and his mother? And if it was the latter, was she ready for that after only just having walked away from Andy?

"I've booked a ticket to Cuba, I'm going travelling, but I'll be back in time for Christmas," Rachel announced quickly before her thoughts could carry her any farther away from her courage.

"I see." Elizabeth was pouring her second glass of wine, the first downed unceremoniously while Rachel had been talking.

"I was hoping, when I return, I might be able to spend more time with Henry. I know it wasn't me he was looking for, he wants to know more about his father, your—" Elizabeth had been busying herself by making the coffee she had offered, but Rachel watched her falter as her late husband was brought into the conversation.

"Alex. His name was Alex."

"But it was me he found." Rachel moved so she could seek out Elizbeth's face, she was finding it hard to continue this conversation with her back.

Rachel stood so her spine was pressed against the counter, fingers wrapped around its top, and to her right-hand side, Elizabeth leaned towards the cupboard in front of her as though she wanted nothing more than just to lean her forehead against it.

"I know I gave him away, I know I have no right to ask you this." She ducked her head so she might be able to search out Elizabeth's eyes, but they were firmly closed. "I would like to get to know him; I think just as he came looking to me for answers, he might be able to help me solve some of my own issues."

"Even though you don't think it was you he wanted?"

"I'm sure Alanis Morissette has a whole verse devoted to us all."

Finally, Elizabeth opened her eyes to look at her.

"Ironic." Rachel tried to smile back at them, trying with the smallest of gestures to transform Mr Bumble back into Elizabeth, not to be thrown into the cellar and told to be grateful for the scraps she was fed.

Elizabeth picked up the coffee she'd made and handed it to her. "Nothing she sings about is ironic. Moronic, perhaps, but not ironic." She picked up her wine glass and turned around. "I'm sure Henry would love a postcard from your travels."

"And you?"

"I'm sorry?"

"Would you like a postcard?"

The glass was quickly returned to the countertop and Elizabeth's hands were rubbing at her eyes. Rachel watched as she removed her earrings and placed them neatly besides the wineglass.

"I appreciate that you drove all the way here to seek my permission, but I am very tired, it has been a long week, and this really could have been conveyed over a phone call."

Rachel was trying to match this woman in the kitchen to the one she had slowly been getting to know, the one that had gone from calling her Ms King to inviting her to share a curry and a night in her home. But once again Rachel was Ms King and invitations to dinner wouldn't come again. Side-lined. Put on a shelf to be forgotten. A distant memory of Henry's childhood.

Do you remember that time I had to pick you up from Dover? Elizabeth might ask one Christmas, after the presents had been unwrapped and the turkey digested. A grandmother might be asleep as the king read through his speech to the nation.

I wanted to meet my birth mother, he would reply. A wife might put a hand to his knee and he would turn and look at her. *Did I ever tell you about that?*

"Was this because I brought up Alex?"

Rachel wasn't an orphan, Rachel was loved.

As Elizabeth walked her wine glass over to the sofa in the corner, Rachel spotted the shadow of Henry's movement in the doorway; she should have known he would have been too curious to stay away.

Henry was loved. Just as she was loved.

She was not about to be thrown into the darkness because she had asked for more.

She crossed the room to join Elizabeth on the sofa, pushing the kitchen door closed as she did so.

"That won't deter him."

"I didn't think it would," Rachel admitted as she removed her shoes so she could sit, as she had the other evening, on her legs, "but it gives me the illusion of privacy."

The illusion that she might be able to stay a little longer in this life.

She pushed her self-doubt away, made herself more comfortable on the sofa.

RACHEL WAS LOVED.

"What's the point, they'll find out everything anyway."

RACHEL. WA—

"They'll?"

"He'll." Elizabeth sat up a bit straighter as if she'd been caught out.

Rachel rearranged herself on the sofa, her back pressed up against the arm, a knee pushing into the cushion. She reached out and put a hand on Elizabeth's thigh. Elizabeth's head turned slightly so she was looking at the hand on leg. Rachel went to pull it back but—

"The roads were wet," Elizabeth's words were slow, deliberate, and Rachel could hear the pain in them, "but that wasn't the issue. We'd lived in this house five years, he knew how to drive, regardless of the conditions. The police knew that. That's not why they came to my door. They didn't want to talk about the roads. They wanted to tell me that Alex had collided with a tree and as the fire brigade freed his body—" Elizabeth placed her hand on top of Rachel's, and she felt the cold of the two metal bands as they came into contact with the tops of her fingers "—because that's all it was by that point. Just a body. Alex was gone."

Elizabeth inhaled and held her breath. "But Alex had been gone for a while. I thought a baby, a son, our son, *my* son, might bring him back. Alex was nervous though, terrified. He'd grown up with his father's moods. That's what he'd called them. Moods. Alex didn't want children in case the moods continued, that they too might suffer the same. As his father had suffered. As he was suffering. Alex had a vasectomy a couple of years before me. He never wanted children." Elizabeth took her hand back and used it to further hide her face.

Rachel had only seen Elizabeth to the highest standard. Even on Sunday morning, when she bumped into her on the landing as they both made their way to the bathroom, Elizabeth looked stunning, not a hair out of place. Yet here, in the dimly lit kitchen, as the autumn night closed around them, Elizabeth's hair was used as a shield. Rachel was not to see her face, not to see her sadness, her tears, her grief and her guilt as she bared her soul.

"As the fire brigade freed his body, the police told me they found a near empty litre bottle of whisky. Scotch. It had to be Scottish. That's what the police wanted to talk to me about that evening when they knocked on my door, my seven-month-old son in my arms. They wanted to talk about the whisky in my husband's car, not the fact that it was wrapped around a tree."

Elizabeth's hand found its way back onto Rachel's. Its wetness causing it to slide along the back of it before Elizabeth squeezed to find purchase.

"When you called me," Elizabeth turned her head, mascara had run down her cheeks, making her skin look so much darker in the cold kitchen, her eyes so much paler in the autumn night, "told me your name and announced that my son was in your flat in Dover with you, I thought this was the moment; all the years I'd forced him to grow up without a father because I just had to have a child, it would all come crashing down around me and he would leave me for you. For his real mother."

Suddenly, she couldn't be near Elizabeth. She couldn't feel her hand on hers. For Elizabeth's hand suddenly felt so much like a hand that had held onto her. This hand belonged to an older woman. In its sixties at the time, it would belong to an octogenarian now. That hand had squeezed Rachel's own, held her tiny hand and explained about moving to Spain. Rachel had been so excited, she had never been to Spain, never left the country. She knew about passports, and those machines in supermarkets where people would disappear behind a curtain and have their picture taken. She would have her picture taken, she would have a passport, she would go to Spain.

But she didn't.

Sheila the Shih Tzu moved to Spain with Tony and Debbie, her mum and dad. But Rachel stayed behind.

It was at seven that Rachel discovered what it was like to be worth less to a family than a dog.

Perhaps she had been loved by Tony and Debbie, but she had been loved less than Sheila the Shih Tzu.

Otherwise, they would have fought to take her with them.

Otherwise, they would have stayed in England with her if the law didn't allow her to travel with them.

"Enough." Rachel snatched back her hand and was on her feet, the coffee cup in her hand forgotten and tumbled to the floor. "I can't listen to this anymore. Do you hear yourself? Yeah, Alex died, and that was sad, but you lived. You lived, and you loved Henry. You were a mother to him. You gave him, undoubtedly," she gestured around the kitchen, "anything he wanted; but more than that, you gave him love. You. Loved. Him."

Rachel looked around the space and found some kitchen roll, tearing off a couple of sheets before attending to the mess she'd made by her outburst. "You know why he came looking for me?" she continued, staring down at the puddle of coffee as it soaked into the paper, she could feel it permeating the thin material and dampening her fingers. "He wanted to make sure that he was good enough for you." She left the paper on the tile of the floor, the coffee had made it useless, and sat back on her heels and resting her hands on her knees. "He didn't care about who I was, per say, he just wanted to make sure the genes I gave him didn't see him returned to me. All any child wants to be is loved. And you did that when I couldn't. He may not have had a father, but in you he had a mother. That's more than he would have got from me."

She looked up at Elizabeth, still cradling a glass of wine in her hands, but now Elizabeth was looking at her again, an unreadable expression on her features, but her gaze intense. What was she thinking? How far off was she when she guessed—hoped—that Elizabeth liked seeing her too? "You were his mother, his father, his family, his home. You were, you *are* his everything." Deep breath. "So, Elizabeth Cole, would you like to receive a postcard from me?"

It seemed to take hours, but then, Elizabeth smiled, and Rachel's heart dislodged from her throat.

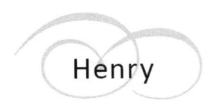

Henry

ALL YOUR MUM ever spoke about was the son she'd have and how she would love him. Caitlin's words rang loud in his ears. Running around his head in a loop. As he slunk down onto the floor, back pressed against the door separating him from his mothers, he stopped hearing the words in Caitlin's voice. He just kept hearing the words until they stopped being words at all. Until they lost all meaning.

He was wanted.

He was loved.

He was the most loved little man in the world.

His mother was tucking him into bed, wrapping an arm around him, whatever book they were currently reading together put gently on the bedside table, the words of the author replaced by her own. *Your father and I, before we were even married, always knew we wanted a little man in our home. I always knew he would be called Henry Alexander Cole.*

But he'd been remembering it wrong. That's not how the story went. That's not the words she created for them as she put him to bed each night. His mother had lovingly crafted different words to guide him into sleep.

I always knew, even before I fell in love, I always knew I wanted to have a son. I always knew he would be called Henry and he would be the most loved little man in all the world.

I always knew, even before I fell in love, **I always knew** I wanted to have a little man in my home. **I always knew** he would be called Henry and he would be the most loved little man in all the world.

I always knew.

It didn't matter that she felt couldn't have had children with Caitlin. It didn't matter that his father had wanted to call him David. Those two things were inconsequential because his mother was always going to have a son, and that son was always going to be called Henry.

Nor, he suddenly realised, did it matter that he was the son of another woman. That the woman had been young and careless. It didn't matter who that woman was because that woman wasn't his mother. That woman had never wanted him. Had never wanted a son. Had never named him before he'd even been conceived.

What did matter though was that that woman was here now. That as he leant back against the door to the kitchen, he could hear this mother comforting his other mother, explaining how important it was that he was loved.

And he was loved.

He was the most loved little man in all the world.

Earlier, as he'd sat beside Caitlin, the radio blaring and the engine pushed to its limits, he'd conjured up the image of a bow. How everything had been tidied up neatly, as if his life were a thirty-minute sitcom, background noise playing as people sat and idled time away on their phones, not paying any attention to the television before them. They might tune in next week, or they might binge it as a boxset, but it wouldn't matter. They wouldn't really be watching. Just as he hadn't really. It had been happening, but he hadn't been paying attention. His mind had been on other things. Perhaps, in this metaphor, he too had been fixated on his phone—too busy googling the actresses, tracking them down on IMDB to work out where he recognised them from; perhaps he'd been on Wikipedia to find out if the story was an original or if it had been adapted from a book, or maybe it was linked to true events and the Executive Producer had fictionalised their own life—only when the end credits started to appear would he realise he'd missed it.

He thought about jumping to his feet, he imagined it all: he would crash into the next room, he would be breathless with excitement, his mothers would look up at him, both lessening their embrace as their wet eyes blazed with their undivided attention to him, and that would be when he would tell them the meaning of it all. Suddenly his voice was Hugh Grant's at the end of *Love Actually*, his mothers were no longer hugging on the floor of the kitchen but clinging on to each other for dear life as they saw each other again at the arrival lounge at any airport in the world. In this imagining he wasn't there at all, he was just a disembodied narrator as he told the audience of the overriding theme of the film. That it was love. That it had always been love.

But instead he just sat there. Waiting for his mothers to emerge, hoping that they would realise that the point hadn't been for him to find love, because he had always been loved, as he would always be loved, but for his mothers to let go of various pieces of guilt they kept locked away inside of themselves—hiding them away for a rainy day of self-loathing and doubt—and accept the fact that they too could be loved, as they themselves loved.

Epilogue

Elizabeth

THE DOOR HAD barely closed behind her when she heard Henry's feet hammering down the stairs. She closed her eyes as she slipped off her heels and silently counted to ten, swallowing back the command not to run in the house. Henry was in the porch with her by the time she'd got to four.

He was beaming, her annoyance with him forgotten.

"And hello to you too." She smiled back at him, searching amongst the shoe rack for her slippers. "Good day at school I take it?"

"Alyssa had a dunker for lunch, Mr Goodman yelled at me for swearing at a Year Seven, and I learnt about family diversity in sociology." He listed the items out on his fingers.

"I understood only two of those points." She smiled back at her excited child trying to lead him into the house proper. "But I expect you could have led the class on family diversity."

"Nah, Craig—you know Craig?—his dad came out when he was four," Henry was talking a mile a minute as he dutifully followed her into the kitchen, "he's now living in Brighton with a man, and his mum's now married to an Indian guy. He kinda dominated the conversation."

"I didn't think Craig took sociology."

"He doesn't." Henry looked at her as if that was entirely irrelevant, jumping up onto the counter as she headed to the fridge. "I got a postcard from Rachel today."

Rachel.

She counted to ten again. Each number trying to steady her heart beat.

Rachel had texted her from Heathrow, asking after their full address and postcode. *Want to make sure the postcard arrives.* She'd closed the message once more with a unicorn emoji, though there had been no umbrella this time. It had taken Elizabeth a couple of days to pluck up the courage to talk to Caitlin about it; she was unsure why she didn't ask Henry, but she reasoned with herself that she wanted Rachel's postcard to be a surprise.

Oh, Rachel texted me the other day, she'd said as they were closing their telephone conversation.

Caitlin had made some noncommittal noise in return, but asked, *How is she?* nonetheless.

She's on her way to Cuba for a couple of weeks, wanted to know our address so she could send Henry a postcard. Do you know why she finishes her texts with a picture of a unicorn?

I knew you hadn't watched that TV programme. Caitlin had sighed before ringing off.

"Yes?" She turned to face him and found him rearranging himself, so he could pull something out of his back pocket. "She went to Cuba, right?"

"Yeah, said the weather is good, she sent you something too."

Another count to ten. Another attempt to slow her heartbeat before she closed the fridge door and moved closer to him, taking the now battered envelope from his hand.

"What's yours say?"

"If you let me open it," she swatted him away as he craned his neck to watch her discover her own postcard, "I might tell you."

She looked at the picture, a 1930s pinup girl with fruit in her hair and a drum between her thighs with confusion, before flipping it over to read the words.

It occurs to me, as I sit on this beautiful beach trying desperately hard not to objectify all these scantily clad women, that I owe you and Hen a home-cooked meal. Fancy it? Where the lines were printed for an address to be written, Elizabeth discovered a closing line: The envelope was to give me the illusion of privacy.

You and Hen, rather than Hen and you.

She thought of the unicorn emoji, she wondered who else had messages closed with such an image. She tried to remember all the TV programmes Caitlin had told her to watch, Caitlin's evenings filled with Netflix while waiting for Matt to return, that might give her clue as to the unicorn. She'd have to watch them all, under the guise of bonding time with Henry, before Rachel got back. Perhaps she'd start with *Wynonna Earp,* that seemed to be the one Caitlin had spoken about most. Henry had already made her watch *Game of Thrones,* but there had yet to be a unicorn in that one.

"Well?" Henry tried to snatch the card away from her.

Elizabeth held it out of his reach, or rather, kept it with her. She finally allowed herself a small smile as she scanned the words again. "Rachel merely says that she looks forward to seeing us upon her return."

And she looked forward to seeing Rachel.

###

About The Author

Kate lives in the south of England with her wife and cat, she spends her time reading, over thinking, and occasionally teaching history to anyone that will listen.

Upcoming

Serena J. Bishop - Dreams

Aurora's life is perfectly mundane. She has a job she hates, an ex that ran her out of her hometown, and the highlight of her week is Monday breakfast with her best friend. That changes when Aurora starts dreaming of a woman who can't remember her own name. A woman who Aurora falls head over heels for. She knows the romance that develops between them isn't real, but the dreams make life so much better that she hurries to bed every night...until she discovers that her dream woman isn't imaginary. Her name is Leela and she is in a coma.

Aurora must risk everything—her job, apartment, friends, and her sanity—to save Leela, a woman she's only ever met in her mind. But in order to help, Aurora must convince Leela's neurologist and parents that she and Leela have a bond that transcends the physical plane.

Can Aurora fight through a progressively nightmarish landscape to wake Leela? And if Leela wakes, will she recognize Aurora as the one who saved her? As the one Leela said she loved? Their dream-relationship might not be real, but if there is any possibility of making her dreams come true, Aurora has to try.

Publishing date: September 10th 2019